TEACHING ABOUT AGING

Religion and Advocacy Perspectives

James B. Boskey
Susan C. Hughes
Robert H. Manley
Donald H. Wimmer

UNIVERSITY
PRESS OF
AMERICA

TABLE OF CONTENTS

PREFACE

This work consists of two separate syllabi and related materials in the field of aging. It has received significant support in the form of a grant from the Administration on Aging, U. S. Department of Health and Human Services. The grant was administered by Dr. Emma Quartaro, Chairperson of the Department of Social Work at Seton Hall University and Director of the University's Multidisciplinary Certificate Program in Gerontology. Initial work on the syllabi was completed in September 1979 but updating has proceeded to the present, especially with reference to bibliographic materials. Both syllabi have been utilized in undergraduate course offerings at Seton Hall. Robert Manley, with the assistance of Susan Hughes, has had overall responsibility for publication of this work, including coordination of the manuscript.

The authors would like to express their warm appreciation to Dr. Quartaro for her valuable advice at all stages of the work.

Margaret Hughes has shown great dedication in typing its final version and Helen Hudson, Production Editor of the University Press of America, has made important contributions to format and final publication phases.

With special reference to the Policy, Law Advocacy and Aging materials, the authors would like to acknowledge debts of gratitude to: Donald Fowles and Joan Shelton of the Administration on Aging, Department of Health and Human Services, Washington; Ronald Muzyk and Dawn Reinke of the Division on Aging, New Jersey Department of Community Affairs, Trenton; Nancy Vvancik, Milton Feinberg and Ronald Heim of the New Jersey Federation for Senior Citizens, Trenton; The Intra-University Program in Gerontology, Rutgers University, New Brunswick; Vicki Gottlich, Institute of Law and Aging, George Washington University National Law

v

Center, Washington; Karen Talty, National Public
Law Training Center, Washington; and to Stuart
Greathouse and Margaret Kraunaur of the Andrus
Gerontology Center, University of Southern
California, Los Angeles.

July, 1982
South Orange, New Jersey

A MODEL CURRICULUM ON RELIGIONS AND AGING*

By

Donald H. Wimmer

INTRODUCTION

Two qualities, a will to live holistically and a strong determination for self-help, both physical and spiritual, are extremely important for the survival and well-being of the elderly. In addition, these and similar qualities in the elderly are important for enabling us to keep service systems within manageable and budgetable proportions. These qualities stimulate the inner dynamics, the subjective factors of living: how one looks on life, what one looks for from life, or feels life is all about. These qualities, whether they are called religious, spiritual, humanitarian or humanistic, constitute the object of study in this A Model Curriculum on Religions and Aging (MCRA).

As a model, MCRA is a working hypothesis, not a perfect ideal. As a curriculum, MCRA is a carefully designed course of study, not a series of topics in a subject area. Its audience includes those who serve the elderly as well as the elder themselves.

*The materials contained in this Model Curriculum are dedicated to John L. McKenzie, a presbyter in the fullest and best sense of the word.

A. Rationale

In the complex world of today, complexity is not confined to technological sophistication. It includes the complexities of the human spirit. Effective and meaningful communication with the elderly requires an understanding of philosophies of life, how they function, and on what levels they are engaged. Understanding how basic values function can enable the gerontologist and the elder to assist in the enrichment of the quality of life of older people. What profit is there in providing a whole world of material services while the elderly suffer the loss of inner integrity?

Life Integration

While gerontology generally engages the social and behavioral sciences along with other academic disciplines to explore values associated with the aging processes, there remains to be explored a field of most basic values, those which give integrity to life by integrating manifold concerns into a unified field of meaning. However vague and indescribable the integration of concerns may be under an attempt to diagram them, integration takes place under the impact of ultimate concern—which may be equally hard to define or describe. Ideally, this is the way religions function. Yet, religions are not automatic formulators or mechanical providers of ultimate meaning and value. It falls upon the shoulders of each individual to put her or his life together. It falls to the gerontologist, as well as to others who serve the elderly, neither to make allowances for the elderly who find themselves struggling in the process, or suffering because they cannot enter into it.

Religions embody and express ultimate values. They convey the traditions that have determined the "age-old" values of societies and cultures. Traditions age as societies age. Traditions are modified as a new values arise. The aging of individuals cannot be unrelated to the aging of society itself. When the individual elderly person consciously or unconsciously experiences the complexities of these changes, a review of life becomes desirable for the sake of peace. Life integration calls for life review.

2

Life Review

Life review requires, among other things, an
awareness of the place that fundamental concerns have
occupied in a person's life and how these concerns relate more broadly to one's religious tradition. Otherwise, there may be unresolved conflicts between what
was learned in early life and what one feels in later
life. Life review is a process of discovering what
one's values have been and are now. Some values turn
out to be relative; others turn out to have been quite
fundamental and ultimate. Ultimate values are embodied
in one's personal religion, which may or may not turn
one of many worldwide. When a person has reviewed
life in this wider framework, he or she can embark
successfully in a project of life review and integration.

"Who knows one religion, knows none." The sensitive and responsive gerontologist, aware of the diversi-
ty of religious traditions and worldviews is able to
serve the elderly with empathy. In this way, religion
is an integral part of any value-oriented curriculum.
This is particularly true for the gerontologist who
seeks to aid persons who have almost completed their
lives and who are now able to view their lives as wholes
in their ultimate dimensions.

Hope v. Depression

To age is to change. Oftentimes, what one learns
about values is that they were products more of society
than of self, for the changes were often induced by
patterns society imposed. It becomes apparent--and
depressing--that many of these are things one would
like to change, but cannot. They are beyond our control.

What is not completely beyond control is meaning.
The meanings we attach to the course of life, the theories which one attaches to aging, have power over an
individual's life. But a person has some power over
the meanings and it is precisely in this power that
life offers hope.

This power has to be exercised over myths that
society induces. One such myth is senility of the type

3

by which society, by misinterpreting normal signs of aging and by falsely attaching non-age-related behaviors to aging, leads millions of people annually into a state of depression about life as a whole.

Since the aged person thinks himself to be senile because he is depressed, he becomes further depressed because he thinks himself senile. Lacking in spirit, he yields himself to death. Being inclined towards sadness, he withdraws from others, spurred by the belief that withdrawal or disengagement is not only socially acceptable but the expected thing to do.

The elderly can overcome these theories by successfully embarking in a project of life review and integration, by discovering what his or her values are.

MCRA hopes to provide some clues as to how this process may be initiated. An essay located in the appendix further provides relections on religion and aging that are of a general nature.

B. Scholarly Literature

An earlier survey by Edward Heenan (1972) reported a mere fifty-five articles and books researching the relationship between religion, death and the aged in "all of the major sociological, psychological, sociology of religion and gerontology journals," i.e, eighty journals in their entirety, plus sixty from 1945-1971.

Heenan grouped research into one category of general works and summaries and four specific categories: (1) organizational participation, (2) the meaning of religion to the aged, (3) religion and person adjustment for the aged, and (4) religion and death.

Heenan's criticisms are as follows: There is no coherent body of literature on the relationships between religion- death and aging. The literature is not cumulative; samples are small and regional. The possibility that religiosity takes new forms among the elderly is ignored. There is a total lack of cross-cultural research on religion and aging. Sociologists of religion possibly do not have the methodological techniques for researching this segment of the population. Gerontologists possibly do not have the methodological techniques for researching religion. There is room for dialogue.

4

Moberg (1965) researching publications to ascertain the perceived role of religion in later years, uncovered contradictory findings. Upon studying contrasting interpretations carefully, he found most opinions colored by religious, a-religious, or anti-religious biases along with great confusion over the meaning of definitions. Atchley (1976) found research on the place of religion in the lives of older people has had very low priority. He does not expect the gap to be filled for some time. Moberg (1978) however, sees spiritual well-being and related issues emerging in the 1980's.

As a movement, spiritual well-being may become a new arena for church-state debate, according to Moberg. Several conferences on spiritual well-being have already indicated its rising importance, not only for sociologists, but also for teachers (Moberg: 1979).

Contemporary spiritual writers are beginning to take note of the need to develop spiritualities of aging. Kilduff (1980), deals with a theology of aging and discusses spirituality of aging. LeFevre and Le Fevre (1981) collected articles by Heschel, Hiltner, Whitehead, rran and Snyder on the theology of aging.

The same collection includes a section on another topic of interest to this curriculum: ministry to the aging. Clements (1981), also provides us with a collection of essays devoted entirely to ministry with the aging. The future promises a steady stream of publications dealing with aging in relation to theology, spirituality and ministry.

C.   The Structure and Design of MCRA

The syllabus is divided into two parts and eighteen units. References are given in each unit, but full bibliographic details are found only in the bibliography, which appears at the end of the syllabus.

The curriculum begins with an examination of what is meant by "religion" and what its role is in culture, particularly with reference to the aging. MCRA then proceeds to examine the major religious traditions of

5

the world, keeping in mind questions of aging. It
would be tempting to put the survey of "religion" in
gerontology literature before the review of the religions
so that the questions on religions and aging would be
clearer and more precise during that study, but to do
so would be to formulate the questions in terms of one
religious tradition. Solutions to problems and answers
to questions depend to a great extent on the formulation
of the problem or question. It may also be tempting to
relegate the study of the religions to another course.
But "religions" are concrete historical phenomena, not
hazy abstractions on the part of the gerontologist or
student of aging. Study of specific religions is better.

The questions of aging that are raised, or the
observations offered, are not claimed to be those raised
by religion, but by the author of the curriculum. MCRA
is designed to familiarize the gerontologist with the
religious experiences of other prople. The student raises
other questions as well. Certainly, as MCRA is implemented in the classroom, new aspects of the aging experience will emerge for discussion and further research. This
is the point at which Part One, composed of Units 1-10,
ends.

Part Two of the curriculum proceeds to explore the
concept of religion as it appears in contemporary gerontology literature. MCRA has been using the concept to
this point as it has been explored in religious studies.
It is necessary to note, for the sake of clarity, what
specific emphases are of concern in the literature and
how they are treated. Qualitative and quantitative approaches are examined. In each case, the differences
due to the different concepts of religion are noted. At
this time, tally should be taken of the ills of the human
condition of the aged. This is to prepare for the next
unit. It is also to ensure that the discussions on religion relate as closely as possible to the real situation.

For "Inhumaneness of Aging," students collect the
tallies taken in the preceding unit and relate them to
the role of gerontology etymologically considered, i.e.,
caring for the old in their weaknesses and vulnerabili-
ties. The students include in their tallies individual
ills and sociologically defined ills, including social
disengagement and the effects of modernization. The
latter stands in greater relief against the background
of the religious traditions; the former requires sepa-

6

rate treatment.

"Religiosity and Disengagement" studies the nature of religiosity, as it is conceived and handled by the literature on disengagement, both individual and social. It is contrasted with Glock's "five core dimensions" and Moberg's sixth core dimension.

In "The Spiritual Dimensions of Aging," features are found that are related to traditional religions in various ways, some ways are obvious, others very indirect. Those that are related to traditional religious themes are pursued here. The remaining ones are taken up in the next unit. They are mostly material conditions for life satisfaction and are spiritual insofar as they function as foundations for sustaining the spirit. Admittedly, the line between this and the next unit is somewhat fluid.

"Life Satisfaction and Life Review" continues to study the quality of life factors which appear in the gerontology literature. It relates in holistic fashion the material and spiritual features. "Spiritual well-being," which appears in the previous unit, is resumed in terms of its religious dimensions. These, in turn, are integrated into the whole range of quality of life factors, setting the stage for "life review." Life review refers to an individual process that examines the assets and deficiencies of each life as it ages. The unit alerts the student against fallacious criteria: centrism, quantification fallacies and the creation of false or unnecessarily restrictive stereotypes.

While the preceding unit relates primarily to the individual, the next unit relates to the communities of faith which are responsive to the material and spiritual needs of the elderly. The subsequent unit relates to the society at large in its concern for its members.

"Religions in Service" studies the communities of faith engaged in rendering services to the elderly. "Communities of faith" are not only churches and synagogues but other not-for-profit organizations serving the elderly. The latter are usually religiously inspired, but without any traditional mandate, either to gain

7

followers or to persuade society to live according to
its religious directives. Nevertheless, their services
to the elderly could be construed - and perhaps should
be - as exercising religious freedom for the good of
others. In most cases, their programs are carried out
with funding from the federal or state government, the
subject of the next unit.

"Church and State in Cooperation" considers the
delicate relationship between communities of faith and
the society at large, as it is related to them through
federal regulation and funding. As programs in aging
develop, church-state challenges are bound to arise.
Proper perspective has to be developed beforehand.
Issues of various natures have to be distinguished from
one another and antecedent models selected (for example,
are military chaplains apt models for cooperation between church and state?). As services to the elderly
become more adequately holistic, the line of separation
becomes more delicate and the cooperation more fragile.

Separation of church and state is to prevent poli-
ticization of people by the churches. It opposes maneu-
vering people who are inept at managing themselves. With
the rise of the "New Generation", it will be more diffi-
cult for non-elders to manipulate the elderly in more
ways than just those that give rise to church-state conflict. This is the subject of the final unit.

"The New Generation" refers to those who will,
upon retirement, become the social critics, responsible
not only for the direction of aid to the elderly, but
also for the redirection of many other activities of
society and of politics. The strong determination for
self-help - referred to in the introduction - will turn
into helping others. The elders need to assert their
authority for the sake of the future of the human race.

This last unit, then, seeks to reform the care-
taker attitude towards the elderly where it should not
be in the programs, and to turn it into an attitude of
caring service, thus affecting the well-being of society
at large.

After the final unit and before the bibliography,
appears an essay illustrating how insights from various

traditions can be integrated in a way that does violence
to none of the traditions.

The format of each MCRA unit is as follows: Under
the heading of the unit is a series of topics which comprise the subject matter of the unit. This is followed
by the body of the unit, a series of comments to initi-
ate and orient the discussion.

D. Aims Goals and Objectives of MCRA

MCRA seeks to appreciate the dignity of aging and
to respect the unique authority that comes with aging
in wisdom and knowledge.

The goal of MCRA is service in an atmosphere of
understanding how older people think and feel as human
beings, not as receptacles into which service delivery
systems pour tax dollars.

The aim of MCRA is to familiarize practitioners
and elders with the humane values of aging in relation to life expectations perceived from diverse worldviews and life views. MCRA studies how life expectations function or can function in contemporary society.
It seeks to offset the demoralizing and depersonalizing
forces of mechanization and fragmentation that acceler-
ate debilitation among the elderly.

The objectives of MCRA are:

(1) To learn about religions so that gerontologists
and elderly alike can evaluate and respond adequately
to human situations affected seriously by religion;

(2) To become familiar with and develop respect for
the variety of religious minorities as well as of
majorities insofar as each serves as a basis and/or
significant conditioner of life values;

(3) To search religions and cultures for those values
which they have attached to aging, in particular, the
relationship between wisdom and old age;

9

(4) To understand religions as they influence human growth and development in the later stages of life;

(5) To develop competency in empathetic appreciation of and sensitivity for the divergent views which other people, especially the elderly, hold with respect to life's ultimate claims;

(6) To estimate the extent to which religions function centrally or peripherally in the life of a given community, especially in relation to aging. Where a life view is generated in which the total sphere of concerns is limited to the secularistic values, this life view becomes, in effect, a religion, and is included;

(7) To appreciate historical and cultural factors which have shaped specific religions and the ways in which these religious groups function in the larger society;

(8) To learn to interact sensitively with elderly people without promoting or inhibiting any religion;

(9) To learn about the religious and spiritual roots of religious intolerance and exclusivism in some of the major and minor religious traditions of the world;

(10) To learn to recognize other limitations and social or psychological ills perpetrated or perpetuated upon the human situation by religions or the abuse of religions, for example: self-righteousness, segregation, vindictiveness in moral values, elitism, bigotry, prejudice and, above all, ageism in any form;

(11) To explore contributions elders can make to their peers and to the wider society.

The aims, goals and objectives of MCRA are proposed with no view to preferring one religion (or non-religion) to another, to suggest any kind of establishment - even "civil religion" - or to manipulate state and federal funds or powers on behalf of religions.

The student does not become a spiritual director

10

applying spiritual solutions to spiritual problems. To
some extent, of course, every truly human interchange
affects the spiritual direction of the other person in
some way. MCRA recognizes this while the student is
learning about the heterogeneous nature of religions,
religious traditions and experiences. While standing
clear of pat answers to religious questions that may
arise in the course of day-to-day encounters, the
student is able to assist the older persons to address
their own questions, deal with solutions that may be
shaped by their own traditions, in short, to find their
own way. He or she helps: to create an environment
compatible with the elder's own (religious) experience
and knowledge, i.e., way of thinking about life; to
treat spiritual dimensions of aging not only as problems
but also as normal phases of life growing towards completion; to recognize problems where they exist and
make appropriate referrals; and, to be of service to
the whole person.

      E.   Perspectives for Studying Religions:
           Methodological Considerations

     Religion is at the heart of a culture. In a
pluralistic country such as the United States, there
are many cultures and many religions. The academic
study of religions, comparative religions or the history
of religions, as it is variously called, is not to be
avoided. It is to be enthusiastically included in
multidisciplinary gerontology studies that wish to pene-
trate the superficial understandings of human concerns
and to enable its students to place themselves empathe-
tically in the situations of others in order·to be of
better assistance to them.

     Not everything pertaining to religion is valuable
or even authentic. Much of it is trivia and "chasing
after the wind" (Qoheleth). On the other hand, much
that seems trivial at first is, under closer examination,
vital and authentic. A degree of academic sophistication
needs to be developed. A moment of insensitivity can
do more harm to an aged person's self-esteem than the
material services provide for life satisfaction.

     The trained gerontologist learns to avoid being
judgmental about the religions of others. He or she
learns to deal with religion-related issues without

entering into affirmations about the truth of falsity of any particular religion, all religions or non-religions.

The term "religion" is used in MCRA in a very broad sense, the way it has been used by the U. S. Supreme Court in rendering judgments in religion-related cases. It, therefore, includes what some would call secular as sacred and as sacred what some would call secular. While Unit 1 of MCRA speaks to the substance of religion in general terms of ultimate values and concerns, it is the functional definition that "works" throughout the course.

In education about aging, careful attention is given to distinguish the study of religion from religious practices, particularly in reference to religious freedom and the public, or in reference to publicly funded programs which have anthing to do with religion. Appropriately the state may not sponsor religious education in the sense of education in a religion. Public funding for education about religions and aging must respect the First Amendment.

U. S. Supreme Court Justice Goldberg said: "It seems clear to me, from the opinions in the present and past cases, that the court would recognize the propriety...of teaching about religion, as distinguished from the teaching of religion." (Concurring opinion, Abington v. Schempp, 1963). If Justice Brennan recognized, as he did, that "It would be impossible to teach meaningfully many subjects in the social sciences without some mention of religion" (Concurring opinion, Abington v. Schempp, 1963), it would be impossible to educate adequately our gerontologists without some assessment of the roles religions have played in shaping the attitudes and lives of the elderly.

In the majority opinion of the same case, Justice Tom Clark noted: "It might well be said that one's education is not complete without the study of comparative religion or the history of religion and its relationship to the advancement of civilization." If education about religions is part of everyone's complete education in the minds of those entrusted with maintaining religious freedom and non-establishment, then it would be consis-

tent with them to state that such a complete education
is more important for those who deal professionally
with persons who, nearing life's completion, long for
life satisfaction in wholeness.

F. Prerequisites

On the part of the instructor, MCRA presupposes
qualifications for teaching religious studies, with
background in world religions, comparative religions
or the history of religions. It is important because
of the tendency to reduce religion to one of its components or to statistical data about it. In the treatment of religions, MCRA does not provide introductory
material. There are more than a few such handbooks in
wide circulation by very respectable authors. One such
should be used in conjunction with the course, unless
the instructor is equipped to present representative
primary source material from the religions. MCRA unit
descriptions presuppose a well-balanced presentation of
each of the religions under study, i.e., a sense of the
value systems cherished by each. This is true also where
MCRA is used in the context of ethics and aging.

The instructor is to judge the length of the units.
MCRA is flexible, so that the curriculum can be adapted
to a variety of program needs, e.g., the level of offer-
ing, relationship to other courses, etc. The curriculum
may be spread over two semesters, for six academic cre-
dits, or more probably, contained within one three cre-
dit course.

On the part of the students, MCRA may be taken as
a first course in religious studies. Course content in
terms of world religions is not so specialized that it
presumes knowledge of the diverse religious traditions,
values and worldviews. Instead, MCRA can introduce them
in a meaningful and specific way. Ideally, it would be
very helpful for the student to have had some background
in at least several religions of the world.

From the standpoint of gerontology, it would be
ideal but not absolutely necessary for the student to
have had a course in social gerontology. MCRA might
also do well as a course preliminary to social gerontology, providing for it an orientation that is value
oriented.

13

G. Student Responsibilities

Assignments and testing depend on the level on which the course is offered academically, the background of the student in both gerontology and religious studies, and on other particular circumstances such as the place of MCRA in the total program.

Generally speaking, two short research papers are recommended to pursue at greater depth historical perspectives and contemporary issues. Readings should be encouraged from selections in the bibliography referred to in the units. For a mid-term and final testing format, the mid-term fits best after Unit 10, which is at the end of Part 1.

PART ONE. RELIGIONS AND AGING
IN HISTORICAL PERSPECTIVE

Introduction

The introductory lecture includes, along with the
usual announcements of texts, office hours, student responsibilities, etc., discussion of the structure and
design, aims, goals and objectives of MCRA and a careful presentation of the perspectives for studying religions in a way in which principles of religious freedom
and church-state separation are not compromised. Even
where the curriculum is incorporated into a theological
program of a particular denomination--indeed, especially there--it is important to avoid confusion since few
aging projects are carried out without some type of
cooperation with state or federal involvement.

Unit 1. The Notion and Function of Religion

Religion: substantive and functional definitions.
Relation to ethnicity and culture. Traditional and non-
traditional religious phenomenon. Spiritual well-being.
Civil religion.

Religion means different things to different people. The term refers to the most fundamental lifeviews,
values and ultimate concerns, i.e., the substance of
religion. Without defining what the substance is--it
varies from each religion--a religion is substantially
present where there is a coherent relationship between
creed, code, cult, community and cosmos (worldview, an
ordered totality). In keeping with "Perspectives" (Cf.E,
p. 10), a working definition that is also a functional
definition is adapted from Clifford Geertz (1973):

Religion is (1) a system of symbols which acts
(2) to communicate values and establish powerful, pervasive and long-lasting moods and motivations in people and strong bonds between them
(3) by formulating conceptions of a general order of existence, and (4) by clothing these conceptions with such an aura of importance that

15

(5) the moods, motivations and bonds are unique-
ly realistic and unconditionally imperative.

The corresponding adjective, "religious", is used
in this broad sense, i.e., not only in reference to
organized religion but especially to ultimate values,
concerns and the meaning of life as a whole.

The symbol system is so powerful that the community finds in it its inner structure for which the social
mores become the cultural manifestation. As the ethnic
group develops, ethnicity provides the supporting framework for the growth and continuation of the religion.
Martin Marty (1972) has called ethnicity the "skeleton
of religion in America." The relation between religion
and ethnicity is especially important in aging studies.

In keeping with the above definition, both traditional and non-traditional expression is given to the
moods, motivations and bonds of religion. This should
not be confused with use of the term "religious" in reference only to organized religion, in which case anything pertaining to a religion is religious, including
its secular qualities! Conversely, many traditionally
religious forms can lose their intrinsically religious
quality. After the world became secularized in the modern era, life itself came to be described and experienced in secular terms. Two spheres of language were
used to describe basically the same phenomenon. Secular
and religious interpretations coincide and the coinci-
dence is no cause for one to reject the other. Thus,
sacred and secular language become mixed in the life
and thought of the elderly. Spiritual well-being to
one is life satisfaction to another. MCRA uses the
language of both spheres because they both refer substantially to the same realities. That is evident from
the literature on aging.

What is called religious here is also called spiritual, although some (e.g., Moberg, 1978) restrict the
use of the former to organized religion. He prefers to
use spiritual well-being. The problem with restricting
religious to organized religion and spiritual in reference to sacred and secular dimensions is the inference
that spiritual well-being dimensions of the secular
sphere are not religious dimensions. This suggests that
no problem of separation of church (religion) and state
exists. Quite the contrary is true. Spiritual well-

16

being as the movement is going presently bears all the earmarks of a "civil religion". In civil religion one finds all the components of a religion in its formative stages. Religious scholars have taken great interest in civil religion of late and a rather large body of literature exists. Though none of it relates that phenomenon to the spiritual well-being movement in gerontology, the connection will not go unnoticed long.

The function of religion in older persons has been hotly debated in the literature, much of it based on whether religion is perceived as organized or not. The Princeton Religion Research Center (associated with the Gallup Poll) surveys opinions, including those on the importance of religion and religious beliefs and on involvement in charity and social services. Statistics show that, in the opinion of the respondents, religion plays a more important role in older age groups and that the largest number of those involved in social service or charity is the oldest group. Should correlation between these two groups show that the same individuals comprise both groups, there is indication that where religious beliefs and concerns are highly cherished there is greater possibility that organized religion can elicit greater portions of the elderly to engage in roles of social responsibility, volunteering their knowledge and experience for the benefit of the total community. This would help restore dignity to aging in America.

Unit 2. Primitive Religions and the Aging

Social status and roles of the elders in primitive societies. Bicameral culture: sacred and secular. Impact of deculturation on the elderly.

General neglect, which led to contemporary problems of aging, are reflected in the lack of interest on the part of religion scholars in the "graying of hair." The lack of rites of passage for menopause or for the graying of hair (van Gennep: 1975) of course eliminates the possibility for studying esoteric rituals. Nevertheless, in primitive societies menopause and gray hair mark the beginning of a new phase of life which is very important. "Old age brings increased social standing." (van Gennep: 145).

According to Gutmann (unpublished paper read in

17

Philadelphia, 1978), a society becomes cultured when
shared values are internalized to the point that they
have a directive effect on the behavior of the members
of the society. Culture appears in societies in which
the sacred and secular are bicamerally ordered. Elders
have prestige and authority (Middleton: 1967). They
preside over the initiations. They render judgments
that guide the life of the community.

When the bicameral balance is upset, deculturation
sets in; the aged become the victims. In a cultured
primitive society, elders, devoid of pragmatic power,
become a fit complement to the community by being ves-
sels of sacred power which elders make available to it
and to its eco-system, so that rain may fall, crops may
grow, etc.

Gutmann continues, describing the traditional professions in our own society, by showing how ethical norms
and pragmatic norms arise. "When the older practitioner
speaks," he says, "he may not be au courant with the
latest techniques, but this historic distillate of the
profession announces itself through his words. The
older practitioner is best qualified to carry on the
moral business of the profession because, for better or
for worse, he has already made his mark: he has no career to build at the expense of others."

Degradation of the elderly is a symptom of deculturation in society as a whole. By concentrating on the
troubles of the aged, we may deny the common tragedy,
deculturation. We better realize their problem is our
problem and work with them, not on them, in establishing
some new social basis in which their potential can be
maximized in meeting our common problem.

Unit 3. Hinduism and Aging

Topics: Absolute reality. Self and reality.
Stages in Life: Retirement and Moksha.

In primitive Hinduism, as elsewhere, elders were
the carriers of social and religious norms. It comes
as no surprise then, that prominent themes make better
sense when they are heard as from the lips of the sages,
the wise elders. Like good wine, their point of view
was aged.

Absolute Reality (Brahman). Older people have
seen many things pass before them which were clung to
as if they were ultimate. Aging lends validity to the
Hindu conviction that what is seen is insubstantial,
transient. Its apparent reality is deception; it is
illusion (maya). True knowledge (veda) is not about
these superficial appearances but about that which underlies it. "What cannot be spoken with words, but that
whereby words are spoken: Know that alone to be Brahman,
the Spirit; and not what people here adore." (Kena
Upanishad, J. Mascaro, trans.). To things, the Hindu
says "Neti, neti" (not this, not this), but tadekam
("that one thing" or "that which is", Rig Veda X. 129).
The aged wisely let many things pass unnoticed because
they are not worth noticing.

Self (Atman) and Reality. In America, the older
adult experiences loss of social and psychological contact with others. Loneliness begins to weigh heavily
on the individual. In Hinduism, "Individuality" is a
gross misunderstanding of reality. One appropriately
withdraws to "the Beyond that is within." Basic beliefs
prevailed according to which one strips away all those
things which make any particular self unique and susceptible to isolation. False "selves" are eliminated in
time by means of disciplined practices (yoga). The
Hindu learns to eschew pursuits of this world and even
interest in one's own existence. Through detachment the
true self, atman, gradually opens before him or her.
Old age is, or should be, a process of detachment from
the superficialities of selfhood and attachment to the
true self which is Brahman.

Stages in Life: Retirement and Emancipation. Hinduism offers an alternative life view to ageist-caused
frustration after mandatory retirement. Life is seen to
progress through stages. In the beginning, the person
is initiated into life. He or she receives everything:
food, shelter, learning and culture. This is the stage
of "initiation". The second is called "householder",
what we call "breadwinner". Here, the Hindu becomes the
provider, a socially productive and responsible individual. It is a busy time. Practical policies are developed
and pursued.

In the third stage, that of retirement, the Hindu

19

withdraws from the busy life of the producer and provider to pursue a highly respected life role. By this
time, life experiences have distilled into a philosophy
of life. The wise old man becomes a source of wisdom
for his younger cohort. He or she contributes to society the values in which the young are initiated and
according to which the householders guide their practical
policies.

The stage of retirement is invested with high value in Hinduism. The retiree is an authority on the art
of living. His role is that of a sage in traditional
societies.

In the fourth stage, variously called emancipation
or liberation (moksha), or preparation for this stage,
prevents the third stage from becoming too absolute,
just as retirement prevents the absolutizing of the work
ethic. In this phase, the person is freed from all the
bonds that bind it to ephemeral concerns. The fourth
stage faces the challenges of increasing vulnerability
and frailty. In it, a person gives up longing for useless things long before the physical support system requires them to do so.

Hinduism's third and fourth stages raise questions
of values and ethics of the individual, questions which
would, perhaps, be taken up earlier in life were they
raised earlier in life. Third and fourth stages are
stages of life review. (Strictly speaking, what is
said here under the fourth stage should be referred to
as anticipations of the fourth stage in some instances.)
Moksha as life satisfaction is the yielding, perhaps, of
the "life satisfaction" the West perceives materially,
for life satisfaction is the final absorption of Atman
into Brahman.

Unit 4. Buddhism and Aging

Topics: The four passing sights. Life and experience: anicca and anatta. Nirvana: the surrendering of
desires.

The passing sights: Young Prince Siddhartha Gautama
of the Sakyas (560-480 B.C.), a member of the administrative caste (the warrior caste, the Kshatryas), first
appears as the picture of the denial of aging. His

20

father, king of a small kingdom, provided nothing but
the best for him. What was not pleasing was removed
from Siddhartha's world. The royal road to success and
pleasure was to be his lot. He would pass through each
stage of traditional Hindu life. But then he stumbled
upon the "facts of life". One fine day he saw an old
man. This was the first of four visions, as they have
come to be called. Aging became a fact: youth is a
passing phase. The three following visions merely complete what the vision of aging started. For the healthy
man, aging changes a person gradually. The sick man is
changed rapidly, and the dead man is changed completely.
To these, aging happens automatically with a weakening
effect. To the monk, who wears the saffron color to
symbolize death, the debilitating aspects of aging are
acceptable. Moreover, the monk actively undertakes to
transform his life while aging is going on in such a
way that the end result of spiritual aging is in harmony
with physical aging.

The monk drops all pretense of preserving youth,
beauty, and strength. These are ignored in the prefe-
rence for a way of life that is disciplined to look at
life as a whole. The monk has reviewed life and, having
evaluated his quality of life requirements, proceeds toward life satisfaction.

The Buddhist perspective is one which rejects the
traditional Hindu stages of life. The monk is a retiree
in effect. Long before old age, he lives as a sage. The
Buddha anticipated the meditation of old age.

Life and experience: Elderly people who have put
in years and years of hard effort are often disgruntled
when life is harsh to them. Buddha, after years with
the ascetics, decided to sit down under a tree until he
found the key to order in his life. He arose enlightened
to say he found it. Life, he said, is dukkha, out of
joint, literally. His insight into the nature of reality is that there is no central balancing feature. The
Buddhist does not expect everything to "fall into place."
Aged people - which is what everyone wishes to become -
must learn that things will never fall into perfect order, not in the present condition.

While we can identify with dukkha, there are other

Buddhist experiences of life which are less easily
grasped convincingly, though we can learn from them.
The Buddhist experience of life is that it is evanescent,
impermanent. Whatever is, will not be. A person should
never make himself or herself at home in the present
situation. Westerners who have learned to make themselves at home in the world, when they age often complain
that things are not what they should be, not what they
were. Life is anicca, everchanging, impermanent, according to the Buddha.

Life is also "insubstantial," anatta, especially
when it comes to such things as "selfhood" and "other."
Westerners' self-experience is one of a "self" to which
things happen or which communicates with others. We make
much of this notion, too much, in fact. The price is
paid in old age with the consequent feelings of loneliness and isolation. We need physical presence. The
Buddhist learns that this kind of need is based on what
to him or her is a false premise, the substantiality of
self. If the elderly are frustrated because they do not
experience the fullness they expected, the Buddhist would
point out that the fulfillment is not in the nature of
human living. In place of the paths of desire we pursue,
the Buddhist proposes a path of no-desire.

The path of no-desire leads ultimately to the ex-
tinction of desire, the highest state a human being can
seek. This is nirvana. This path is one of liberation
from the bonds that bind us, our desires. Desires bind
us to the past which no longer exists, nor will exist.
A wise elder is one who learns to unburden the self from
desires which bind it to a past that cannot be realized.
To reject these desires is to leap toward the fulfillment the Westerner is headed for. A fulfilled life is
one in which there are no unfulfilled desires. Buddhism
provides one way of eliminating those desires. While
this may be a very pragmatic approach for the elderly,
it is an ideal to be pursued earlier in life.

Unit 5   Religions in China and Aging

Topics: Ancestor worship. Age in the five great
relationships, according to Confucius. Li, Hsiao.

Ancestor worship is variously understood. Some-

22

times it is near magic based on fear. At other times,
it is devotion based on love. At the heart of it, is
the cherishing of values of the oldest type. Ancestor
worship is, by no means, restricted to China; it is
everywhere (i.e., common). But in China it developed
in a very articulate way, due to the editing of the
classical traditions by Confucius (551-449 b.c.).
Through the ancestors, the values are realized and held
up before the younger generations. When they are thus
internalized, a culture arises to carry them forward in
specific historical forms. This can be illustrated in
this country by referring to the "Faith of our Fathers."

While the worldview of Hinduism and Buddhism is
drastically different from our own, that of China is
not so strange. While the two preceding religions offer advice for the frail and vulnerable elderly, the
wisdom that China offers is of benefit to the social
status of the elderly and to a more positive or active
role for them in society.

In creating the Deliberate Tradition by editing the
classical literature, Confucius singled out five great
relationships which depict the dominant relationships
in life. Unlike the Realists who say there is no value
in human relations under stress, and unlike the Mohists
who place great value on love indiscriminately bestowed
on all alike, Confucius found a middle way. The conviction of Confucius was that love alone is not enough.
Other humane qualities are required for an orderly and
peaceful community. He identified five great relationships and, in addition, pointed out that in each relationship there are two sides, e.g., the relationship
between ruler and subject: The ruler shows benevolence
and the subject shows loyalty. Between friends, too,
there is a difference, and the difference, interestingly
enough, is age. The same difference is found between
brothers. It is not that the older has privileges the
younger does not have, though undoubtedly that is the
way it worked out often enough. Each has its obligations.
The younger brother is respectful but (and) the older
brother is gentle. The younger friend is deferential;
the older friend is considerate.

To learn from Confucius is to learn that false
equality exists by refusing to recognize the differences.

23

Older people have different needs and different obligations than younger people have. But always, the older
people receive respect.

Those special elders to receive respect are parents.
Hsiao, filial piety, is an inward respect or reverence
which goes especially to parents. It was generalized
to include all sorts of elders and even all that was
ancient or archaic.

Confucius offers a word applicable to gerontologists and all who serve the elderly. "Tzu Yu asked about
filial piety. Confucius said:'Nowadays a filial son is
just a man who keeps his parents in food. But even dogs
or horses are given food. If there is no feeling of reverence, wherein lies the difference?' " (Analects II,
7).

Respect for the elderly is good form, propriety,
or Li. "Li is based on heaven, patterned (copied) on
earth, deals with the worship of spirits and extends to
(everything)... Therefore, the sage shows the people
this principle of a rationalized social order and through
it everything becomes right in the family, the state and
the world." (Li Chi, IX). The sage is the one who communicates the values of life; he has a responsible role.
This teacher, of course, does not fail to communicate the
values of and respect for advanced age.

Unit 6. Aging and the Ancient Near East

Topics: Mythic beginnings: in illo tempore.. Primitive democracy in ancient Sumer. The Mesopotamian king
list. Gilgamesh. Wisdom and the elders.

Throughout the world, there are myths of origins.
Often enough a return to origins is a denial of aging
(Eliade: 1954). Generally, however, the entry into mythic
time is an atemporal experience. In illo tempore (at
that time, in the beginning) the gods displayed their
greatest power. That time is creative, vital; its re-
enactment is a return of the most immense of realities.
The regular appearance of mythic time in profane time
represents a new begimning with a reassertion of the
vital forces intact. But reactualizing illud tempus does
not represent a denial of aging. It has no relation to
it essentially. On the other hand, illud tempus is

24

imagined in terms of very long periods of time. Historical times that are more closely associated with origins are thought to be longer than later epochs.

Sumer, the oldest Mesopotamian civilization about which there is any clearly defined body of knowledge, brought its people into the historical period. At the most ancient phase and probably also in the prehistorical phase, the city was governed by a body of elders who only in times of emergency selected one of their number to serve as king for the limit of the emergency. Though it is not clear that only older people served in this capacity, it is clear that the prestige of the office came through association with age (Jacobsen: 1946).

An illustration of the thesis that the closer a period is to the origins the longer the lifespan is found in the Mesopotamian king list (ANET, 265). This means that, for all those who preserved this and similar traditions, aging was not viewed negatively.

Nor does the Epic of Gilgamesh view it as such, except at one critical point later on in the story. The walls of Uruk rest upon foundations laid by the sages, i.e., men of knowledge and experience, older men. This feature is brought to attention at the very beginning and again at the end of the epic. Seeing the death of his close friend Enkidu, Gilgamesh seeks to ask questions about life. They are, in a word, about aging. Utnapishtim tells Gilgamesh about the plant that will restore lost youth to a man. Gilgamesh plans to take it to the old men to eat. Its name shall be "The Old Men are Young Again", he says. He lost the plant and had to return to Uruk and accept his fate. One could say that to accept aging is a major theme, for in the closing comments on him is the saying: "The heroes, the wise men, like the new moon have their waxing and waning" (Sanders: 1972).

Perhaps the most relevant topic is the wisdom tradition in the entire ancient Near East. Wisdom rests on belief in the validity of human experience (McKenzie: 1965). One gains knowledge in the art of living by learning from experience, hopefully the experiences of others. It takes time though time does not provide it automatically. A youth is a fool by definition (i.e.,

25

not a wise man because he lacks the experience). An old
man should be wise. Hence, the saying: There is no fool
like an old fool.

The ancient Near East does not idolize old age.
It recognizes its debilities. Part of its wisdom is
on how to live as a wise man, i.e., an old man.

Unit 7. Aging and the Old Testament

Topics: Elders. Genesis 1-11. Patriarchs. Psalm
71:9-10. Proverbs. 1 Samuel 12. Ecclesiastes. Leviticus.
Wise men.

The term "elders" in the Old Testament applies in
all but a few places to a social role of a group and
not merely to "old men" (McKenzie: 1959). They are
usually associated with the leadership of the community.
Chronological age by itself was insufficient.

The prehistory of Genesis 1-11 is the story of
a decline and the spread of sin. As sin spreads, the
lifespan is shortened.

Patriarchs live to a ripe old age, although it is
shorter than their ancestors in the prehistory. To be
"full of days" is to complete a fulfilled life. To be
old is to be blessed.

The life of the old is as entrusted to God as it
was during youth. This is the theme of Psalm 71. The
old seek support from God for two reasons against the
vulnerability of old age. "Society" has those who are
ready to take advantage of him or her (Ps 71:9-10).
More positively, the old need support in order to pro-
claim all the wondrous deeds God has done for them from
youth (Ps 71:17-20). Verses 21-24 suggest a retirement
time of testimony to a life of favors.

Biblical wisdom frequently refers to the honoring
of age, Proverbs 20:29, and Wisdom 2:10, for example.
Sirach 6:34; 25:4-6 is especially important in the praise
of wisdom, experience, judgment and fear of God of the
aged. See also, Proverbs 30:7-9, 17.

In Samuel's address to all of Israel in 1 Samuel

26

12, his speech is based on his own integrity and his integrity on his life-long uprightness. He swears by it, and the people accept what he has to say. As Job 12:12 says: "With old age is wisdom."

The advise of Ecclesiastes, however, is to avoid making old age an ego trip. The wisdom of man does not have in it the wisdom to overcome evil (Ecc. 8:17). It recognizes that old age can be "evil" and with no pleasure (Ecc. 12:1, especially).

Nevertheless (or perhaps, therefore) the Holiness Code of Leviticus states that the young are to "Stand up in the presence of the aged, and show respect for the old" (Lev. 19:32).

Respect for the old is not based on chronological age. The older person is to be respected for his or her knowledge and experience expressed in wise judgments. The wise person is, in a sense, self-made. This person has mastered collective wisdom. Wisdom begins by listening to one's elders. McKenzie (1974) presents a well-rounded treatment to which the reader is referred (pp. 203-231). His discussion relates wisdom in the Bible to the previous unit's theme in the ancient Near East.

Unit 8. Aging and Judaism

Topics: Honoring one's parents. zāken. Rabbinic literature.

Parental homage runs deep in the Jewish tradition. One's parents are one's elders. They play the role that the older cohorts play in society, but with greater love, care and devotion. However, respect is due because they are parents, not because they are older.

Often overlooked is the clause attached to this commandment. The Epistle to the Ephesians (Eph. 6:2) calls it the first commandment with a promise. It is more like the first commandment with a veiled threat (cf. Dt. 5:16; Ex. 20:12). Deuteronomy 21:18-21 explains what happens when the commandment is violated. Note the role of the elders at the city gates (the proper place of official business of this kind). The

27

guilty son is to be stoned by the citizens after a trial
by the elders. Exodus 21:17 orders death to the son who
curses his parents. Leviticus 20:9 explains why: He
who curses his parents has forfeited his life. The
promised reward for observing the fourth commandment is
nothing else than old age as a fulfillment of life.

Zāken is a word well worth studying thematically
in the Old Testament with reference to early Judaism.
In the singular, it meant "old man", usually, but in the
plural, it usually meant "elders", those with authority
as a collectivity. In Jeremiah 26, representatives of
the elders of the land come to Jeremiah's defense. These
are obviously representatives, i.e., not all elders pre-
sided, else there would be no head of the community.
Time sees the elders only of certain families eligible
for government (Bornkamm: 1968). These elders become
the supreme ruling body in the Jewish community in
Persian times. Eventually the "Council of Elders" becomes the Sanhedrin, but by the first century of the
Common Era, "elders" are the weakest group of the three
components of the Sanhedrin.

Among the scribes, where wisdom is cherished deep-
ly, scholars are the wise men. In distinction from the
broader term for wise, hākām, is the honorary title bestowed on older scholars, zāken. But by the time of
rabbinic literature, this title is applied to ordained
scholars.

In rabbinic literature, there is a "poignant counter-
point between the growth in wisdom and learning that is
achievable only with age, and the physical decline
characteristic of old age" (Clingan: 1975). The Synagogue Council of America published in its guide to aging
programs for synagogues numerous excerpts from rabbinic
literature establishing the link between the needs
characteristic of the weakening of old age and act of
kindness as religious acts.

According to the rabbis, oldness by itself is no
virtue; wisdom and knowledge of the Torah determine its
value. Full mental and physical powers are sustained
through dedicated study of the Law.

Unit 9. Aging and Early Christianity

Topics: The Novum. Greek Terminology. Greek
patristic literature.

While Christianity continues in the tradition of
the Old Testament as far as values and obligations are
concerned, there is a feature whose negative impact has
unwittingly caused or at least occasioned much of the
illness of contemporary post modern society. As a cause
it is certainly not intentional, but the effect is
evident nevertheless. It is the fixation upon the new
which is described as the negative impact of the Novum,
or the bypassing of old age values. To be sure, modernization is at the immediate root of modern problems of
aging as we know them today, but there is something of
a preparation for it in older literature.

Theologically, Jesus Christ is the Novum. He is
the new Moses, Giver of the New Law, the New Covenant.
He is the new Adam, the head of a New Creation. Jesus,
depicted in the New Testament as the Wisdom of God,
accomplished the work of salvation at an early age, and
died young. Before him all that is older is seen in its
deficiencies, or so Christianity will begin to interpret
the "old."

The negative impact of the theology of the Novum,
neglect for values of aging, does not begin with the
Novum. It is perhaps as old as the institution of
"elders" when that institution withheld authority from
qualified elders and vested it in a few who then included
personnel not qualified by aged wisdom. But the ideology
of the Novum tipped the balance away from the old.

Among the several terms of aging in Greek, presbyteros and geron are the most relevant to our discussion.
The second term carries negative connotations, emphasi-
zing the weakness, frailty and vulnerability of old
age. Gerontology is appropriately derived from it. It
is precisely the need element which gives rise to it in
the first place. Presbyteros (comparative of presbýs),
on the other hand, "contains from the very first the
positive element of venerability" (Bornkamm: 1968). In
Greek literature, the honor due the old or age is a
favorite theme in popular ethical instruction. In Greek

societies when the term is not used as a title - in
which case it refers to an office (much as our "town
fathers", "aldermen", "senator") - there is rich attes-
tation to them as senior groups of various kinds (as
opposed to junior groups). The Septuagint, incidentally,
prefers presbyteroi over gerontes for zekenim (Bornkamm).

The peculiar problem in both Judaism and Christianity arises from the twofold meaning of presbyteroi.
It is not always clear which meaning is intended. To
be sure, eventually in Christianity the meaning is always in reference to the priesthood. Two observations
need to be made: Aged discernment is the model for
priesthood; and, respect for the elderly calls for a
transfer to them of their presbyteral dignity and authority.

Christian literature, beginning with the New Testament, brings out the patriarchal character of the
presbyterate (1 Peter). In 1 Timothy 5, the reference
is clearly to age, but elsewhere, where elders are ap-
pointed to offices, we may witness that to mature Christian (males) were assigned certain responsibilities. In
time, the responsibilities became identified with the
class (those qualified by experience gained over a period of time) from which the personnel was drawn. The
negative result was that the implication of those not
chosen as being not "worthy". The "remainders" (the
majority) are relegated to the masses of old folks.

In 2 and 3 John, the elder (presbyter) is neither
one of the old folk nor an office holder in a monarchi-
cal episcopacy. He is one of those we meet again in
Papias, Irenaeus, Clement of Alexandria and Origen: a
specially valued teacher, a prophet of the older period
who conveys the authentic tradition.

In 1 Clement, presbyteros is used in reference to
the command to honor the aged. Later in the same letter
it refers to office holders using the same term.

Ignatius sees presbyters as having a fixed place
in the hierarchy. They stand around the bishop as his
council. He does not view obedience as 1 Peter and 1
Clement did, on the command to revere the elderly and
their teachings, but solely on the mystery of the unity
of the Church. But the term still signifies, for other

30

writers (named above), members of the older generation
who are regarded as mediators of the authentic tradition
and teachers. As in Judaism, their sayings are the
"authoritative sayings of the fathers." Christianity
will call the period in history the Patristic Era.

Unit 10. Aging and Islam

Topics: Traditions taken up by Islam. Shirk and
the rejection of priesthood. The elder in Islamic
society. Brotherhood.

Islam accepted in its beginning much that is
common to both Judaism and Christianity with respect
to the wise elder and the honoring of one's parents.
It also was open to these values in the tribal societies
from which its first membership largely came. Therefore,
much would be repetitious.

On the other hand, there were certain things deemed
by Muhammed to be abuses, absolutely the worst of which
was the tendencies of all prior religions to associate
human things with the devine and, by giving them divine
values, rob God of his true uniqueness. This is particularly true of priesthood. No images of God, in human
or animal form, are tolerable. Christian priesthood,
in his view, long infringed on the transcendence of Allah.
Muhammed rejected the priesthood in any of its forms.
The form he knew was highly clericized and not very highly educated. While they took the honorary title (father)
from the "Fathers", they knew little of the All Wise,
the Merciful, the Compassionate. For him, it was the
sacrament of human arrogance.

As time developed, the teachings of the Prophet,
law (figh) and tradition (hadith) grew up around the
Qur'an. The Qur'an was memorized by "Qur'an bearers"
who recited what they memorized. Teachers, ulama, became attached to mosques, and a tradition of elder-
teachers was on its way.

It might be noted that Muhammed defied one ageist
concept: he married a woman much older than himself,
Khadijah. But far more important in overcoming ageism
(or preventing it) is Muslim teaching that all who accept Allah as the one and only God, and Muhammed as his
prophet are brothers.

31

Ageism has been called the last frontier of prejudice, following racism and sexism. Undoubtedly, there
are other major efforts to come in other areas. But the
conception of universal brotherhood in Islam which is a
strong antidote to the racism found in Judaism and in
Christianity (the same cannot be said about sexism) can
be put to good use in aging. Universal brotherhood
recognizes that the needs of people differ. So do the
needs of older people.

Conclusion of Part One

In studying the literature of and the literature
about the major religions and the traditions of the
major religions, no prominent trace was found of the
problems of aging of the magnitude experienced by
modern societies. While there are prohibitions against
many things, there is nothing to suggest that the aged
are an oppressed or deprived class. The Bible often
looks out for the widow--the orphan and the poor, but
it never includes the elderly as a distinct group. Undoubtedly, many of the widows and poor were aged, but
there was no degradation due to age itself. Therefore,
if the journey through the religions was an attempt to
seek solutions to our problems under the premise that
they were theirs as well, one returns empty-handed. If
on the other hand, the journey was taken with a willingness or openness to recognize by compairson or contrast
the weaknesses in our own socieyt, the sojourner returns
to meet the challenges such as those delineated in Part
Two, with a broadened perspective and a freshness of
approach.

PART TWO. RELIGIONS AND AGING
IN CONTEMPORARY PERSPECTIVE

After learning about the variety of religious
traditions, MCRA turns to a different literature which
has its own perspectives, vocabulary and concerns, Special
attention should be given to the fact that, in many diverse efforts of social scientists and gerontologists to
come to grips with problems of aging, different definitions are at work. This is especially true of "religion."

Unit 11. Religion and Current
Gerontology Literature

Topics: Religion. Two approaches to aging in
general. Role of theory. Sociologists of religion.

The holistic and qualitative view of religion
taken in the beginning of the course is reviewed and
pursued in relation to quantitative approaches to religion. The former is concerned with quality of life
and ultimate purpose, viewing religious practice as the
means of achieving and expressing it, whether society
calls it religious or not.

In gerontological literature, "religion" is given
a different emphasis. Moberg (1978) observed that the
study of the role of religion in human well-being has
been ignored. Religion is usually studied as a means
for verifying other things (e.g., social participation).
The type of literature closest to it in religious studies
is the "scientific study of religion" of the type found
in the journal of the same name.

Quantification, percents and tables are important.
Under these conditions, religion usually means organized
religion. The dominant behavior quantified is church
attendance. Follow-up research tends to embrace other
religious practices of explicit religion, Bible reading,
listening to religious radio and television programs.
Religion viewed in this manner serves the purposes of
MCRA very indirectly at times. Here we seek to inte-
grate the two approaches where feasible.

33

Mannheim (1952) described the two approaches or methodologies brought to bear upon the problems of generations. Thus it is a question of the two approaches to religion where, on the one side, little research has been done and on the other careful interpretation needs to be done.

The two approaches are amply illustrated in a single volume (Van Tassel, ed.: 1979) with Harevan Laslett and Demos on the side of the quantitative approach and with Edel, Fiedler, O'Connor, Erikson and Sayre on the side of the qualitative approach. The second group represents those who rely on the interpretation of human experiences for understanding advanced age while the first group relies on quantitative formulation of factors ultimately determining human existence.

Quantified research is essential for implementing programs that truly serve the common good, i.e., do the most for the greatest number in the most economical way. But quantified research by itself is insufficient. In questions of meaning it easily falls prey to reductionism, reducing the whole to the measured and verified part. Reductionism appears in reducing religion to organized religion and in assigning greater value to lesser (but more easily verfiable) elements.

The value of church attendance, for example, varies from one church to another. To use church attendance as an indicator of voluntary attendance is less applicable to Catholics than it is to Protestants. Lazerwitz (1962) found regarlarity of church attendance represents the religious emphasis of specific religious groups.

Church attendance by itself is no assurance of anything religious. Religion has been saying that from the beginning. Social pressures or emotional selfishness can displace religious motivations.

Nevertheless, gerontology has given currency to the term "religiosity" defined quantatively with reference to church attendance. The high degree of confusion and uncertainty caused by attempting to apply quantification to religious qualities is recognized by at least one author (Atchley: 1977).

Riley (1978) pointed out how theories of aging have power over the life course. Similarly theories or conceptualizations of religion have power over the interpretation of its significance and influence. A distinction between two definitions of religion shows they are not in conflict but how they are complementary to each other: the substantive and the functional (cf. Unit 1). In quantified research, it is the functional aspect of religion that is important. The problem exists as to determining the relative value of functions with regard to specific religions. Some assistance may come from Mannheim and Riley in their concern for the social role of knowledge and the power of ideas.

It is helpful to understand where available data comes from. Fukuyama (1962) showed how, in the early days, American sociologists were closely linked with the leadership of religious bodies where church attendance was of vital importance. This accounts for the heavy emphasis on organized religion in sociological studies of religion (cf. Berger and Luckman: 1969).

Unit 12.   The Inhumaneness of Aging

Topic: Negative features of aging which lead to or follow from aging.

Inhumane aspects of aging are briefly noted and reviewed in order to set the direction for addressing the issues and viewing solutions to problems pursued throughout the rest of the course and in personal research. MCRA chooses this approach because it goes well with the literature, because of the nature of gerontology and, in the view of some (cf. Atchley:1977), the situation of the older people itself is now seen as a social problem.

Inhumaneness includes not only the obvious individual ills of aging: loneliness, isolation, increasing debility of body, mind and heart, lack of food, proper transportation and housing. These are the deficiencies that the elderly experience so acutely and clearly. Inhumaneness also includes socially derived, more acute and subtly applied pains of aging. These are the ones

35

derived from age stratification (Riley, et al.: 1972),
modernization (Cowgill: 1972, 1974a, 1974b), economic
development that produces new occupations that displace
older employees, social disengagement (Cummings and
Henry: 1961) whereby society phases its older members
out of social intercourse by mandatory retirement, individual disengagement subtly applied by society, myths
of senility, inferior institutionalization in nursing
homes and any other form of ageism.

Unit 13. Religiosity and Disengagement

Topics: Voluntary disengagement v. voluntary participation. The meaning of religiosity. Value of disengagement literature.

Disengagement studies verified the fact that society forces individuals to withdraw from society progressively as age advances. Mandatory retirement is
the sharpest and most decisive moment in the process.
The theory of Cumming and Henry (1961) and Cumming
(1964) that individuals wish to withdraw as they age
has largely been discredited in the literature. Mindel
and Vaughan (1978) found that non-organizational participation perhaps does - though this says little about
whether it is voluntary or not.

To draw these conclusions, research had to be done
in terms of statistically verifiable representative cross
sections of society. Where else than in the churches
and synagogues can one find representative cross sections
of voluntary participation? Since physical presence is
a prerequisite for participation in the activities of
the congregation, it can logically be deduced that a
drop in attendance represents a drop in the voluntary
participation in free societies. The label suggested
for this phenomenon was "religiosity." (For the re-
searcher who is detached from religion, mere church
attendance is counted as religiosity! cf. Moberg:
1967 on biases - pro and con - in the scientific study
of religions).

Since physical attendance drops among the older
people, the conclusion was drawn that older people are
less religious. While attention was drawn to the fact

36

that the study merely wished to deal with voluntary participation of the elderly in society, others took to task that religiosity declined. Hochschild (1975) followed by Mindel and Vaughan (1978) argued that one's role as a religious person encompasses more than participation in religious organizations and that it also includes private religious behavior and what else has "meaning" for life. Organizational disengagement is insufficient. Given the nature of many organizations, religious or not, withdrawal is sometimes necessary for genuinely social engagement.

The value of disengagement literature for religions and aging lies in its exploration of the functional dimensions of religion. Though one may disagree with the results, disagreement is more with interpretation of the results of the research than with the results. It alerts the student to what "religiosity" means to social scientists. Since it refers to a single feature of religion and the frequency of its appearance , it should not be taken in its usual dictionary meaning which refers to the quality of being religious, especially of being "excessively, ostentatiously or mawkeshly religious" (Webster) or "affected or excessive in devotion to religion" (Random House Dictionary of the English Language). No amount of statistics, only the interpreter, can say whether the single feature, church attendance, is an indicator of minimal, normal or excessive religiosity. Only one instance suffices to provide the material base for the judgment‼ On the other hand, frequency of appearance is necessary before any phenomenon can be considered a standard or regular feature of something, which in this case, is that, as age increases, church attendance decreases. Follow-up studies (e.g., those cited, plus Bahr: 1970; Moberg: 1965a, 1965b and others, cf. Bibliography, below) have pursued further dimensions of "religiosity" to indicate that the external forms of being religious change in old age. To those who quantify data - as well as those who choose to remain solely with qualitative description - caveats mentioned above apply. There is widespread disagreement among scholars concerning the nature and value of religion in the lives of individuals and in society.

Unit 14. <u>Spiritual Dimensions of Aging</u>

Topics: Core dimensions of religiosity. The use of terms. 1971 White House Conference and its results. Future Planning.

Glock (1962) identified five core dimensions of religiosity: ritualistic, ideological, intellectual (cognitive), experiential and consequential (works). Moberg (1967, 1976) added a sixth which he called the faith dimension or the spiritual dimension. Though social science can study it only indirectly, there is a valid means of appraising it. The spiritual dimension includes the anti-religion stance of the atheist.

A holistic approach seems to require a middle road spiritual dimension is not to be disregarded as irrelevant, as the view opposite to Moberg insists, and it is not an additional dimension in a sense that the five are. The spiritual dimension is what the five core dimensions of Glock manifest.

Essentially, the spiritual needs of the aging are not different from anyone else's. "The spiritual needs of the aging really are those of every person writ large" (Bollinger).

This curriculum uses "religious" as adjectival to "religion" in its organizational and non-organizational senses. David O. Moberg, the leading scholar who is both social gerontologist and sociologist of religion, restricts "religious" to organized religion and includes in it the secular dimensions of organized religion. For him, "spiritual" includes what is secular as well as what is religious insofar as either refers to the well-being of the whole person. Religion scholars would see in his definitions the "American Civil Religion" as it is informally established in government sponsored activities (cf. Richey and Jones, eds.: 1974 on civil religion). The terms, religious and spiritual, for all intents and purposes, may be used interchangeably, in the opinion of MCRA. The instructor should make clear to the student his or her use and understanding of the terms.

38

Spiritual well being, as the term is used in the 1971 White House Conference, "relates to all areas of human activity...to man's inner resources, especially his ultimate concern, the basic value around which all other values are focused, the central philosophy of life --whether religious, anti-religious, or non-religious-- which guides a person's conduct, the supernatural and non-material dimensions of human nature."

Spiritual well-being varies from one religion to another. In some religions the above definition makes no sense at all, but the intent is clear. MCRA strives to preserve the sense of religious pluralism by remind- ing the student that, while there are many religious traditions, the above definition arises from one or two of them and that allowance has to be made by adapting the definition to other religions' conception of whole- ness. One's own religious understanding should be a means for understanding those of others. It should not be imposed upon others.

The Spiritual Well-Being Section of the 1971 White House Conference was an attempt to face up to the pro- blems causing spiritual poverty suffered by the elderly as a result of changes in our society. It recognized that there are needs to be met which are in addition to physical, material and social needs that are provided for in other government programs.

The conference sought not to do the work of reli- gious bodies but to cooperate with them in the discharge of their responsibilities. It stated long-range goals and clarified its assumptions. It concluded with fif- teen recommendations to which were added allied recom- mendations from other Sections of the Conference. Moberg (1978) observed that the conference along with quality- of-life movements evidence the fact that the findings of scientific researchers are gradually beginning to make an impression.

Moberg defines the areas of impact as:
1. Cooperation of government with religious bodies
2. Chaplaincy services

39

3. Evaluation of government-sponsored programs
4. Home care services
5. Multiservice community centers for older persons
6. Dignity in dying
7. Tax exemption status of non-compliant churches
8. Spiritual care of minorities
9. Licensing of therapists
10. Christian social ethics

Involvement of the state in some of the impact areas is bound to give rise to court challanges, but this is no excuse for avoiding the problems of the aged. Activities should be planned in advance to avoid unnecessary challenges.

Planned activities should include at least the five following components (Moberg):

1. Spiritual well-being as the focus
2. Value clarification
3. Value implementation
4. Research
5. Education

Spiritual well-being should not be considered to be exclusively the domain of religion. Value clarification in a pluralistic context means that all persons work upon their own value systems in the context of emerging issues. Pluralism does not require watering down faith, but expressing it for the benefit of all. Value implementation means not only following faith with works. It means following through with works in all needed areas of life including health, housing, etc. Spiritual well-being is a complicated subject which pertains to subject matter from all the humanities, social and behavioral sciences and numerous applied disciplines and fields of study, especially social work, psychiatry, counseling and pastoral care. The needs of the aging are the needs of all, writ large. Perhaps, but the ways in which these needs are met require special attention at this point in history. Remedial and preventive education is the final component in any designed program.

Education is to include the sensitive issues of religious freedom, separation and the offspring of these two: voluntaryism. Solutions voluntarily undertaken which respect the primacy of the worth of persons is eminently preferable to solutions imposed from above by the dominant idology, group or institution.

Unit 15.   Life Satisfaction and Life Review

Topics: Quality of life. Material and physical needs. Non-material needs. Life review. Remembering. Pitfalls: "life-course," "age reification," "cohort centrism," "quantification," "senility." Life closure.

Spiritual well-being as it is developing seems to fall under the religious tradition that is still emerging and is yet to crystalize fully: the American civil religion. Other research on the quality of life stays away from it. Meeting material necessities of older people is the object of its attention.

The needs are identified as health, nutrition, clothing, shelter, and in our complex society these items take many forms. Surveys support conflicting conclusions. Some arguing for guaranteed income, have "proven" that economic stability is the basic need. Lower life satisfaction of the recently retired resulted primarily from the loss of income and not from the loss of worker-producer role. Higher incomes reduces the impact of health programs on life-satisfaction (See Chatfield, 1977).

A better approach is in a study by Larson (1978) measuring life satisfaction against earlier expectations. From a list of ten variables he found fulfillment in these categories was generally greater than expected.

If the assumptions behind such studies is as it seems to be that meeting material needs gerates life satisfaction, these studies reflect values at odds with most traditions of mankind, except for recent materialistic ones. If the assumption is what it does not appear to be that these are but material dimensions of spiritual well-being, then, they are basically in accord

41

with the perspectives of MCRA. In either case, they have informational value, even if philosophical disagreement is encountered.

Flanagan (1978) identified fifteen factors defining quality of life. Only the first two categories, "material well-being and financial stability" and"health and personal safety" relate to the above studies. Other categories are: "Relations with spouses (girlfriends or boyfriends)," "having and raising children" "Relations with parents, siblings, or other relatives," "relations with friends," "activities related to helping or encouraging other people," "activities relating to local and national governments," "intellectual development," "personal understanding and planning," "occupational role," "creativity and personal expression," "socializing," "passive and observational activities."

Life satisfaction implies some sort of life review, formal or informal, explicit or implied in recalling the past. Practically speaking, it involves letting go of projects whose completion is no longer necessary. There is a sorting out of priorities and a taking control over life's details. Aging in these activities does not diminish the spirit, it enhances the spiritual powers by focusing them on achievable goals or on achieved goals in a reminiscence of fulfillment. Care must be taken lest remembering deteriorate into depression.

Life review is not just a week-end retreat, though it may begin there. It usually begins with pre-retirement planning and continues throughout retirement. Future life expectations are sorted out and sized-up. Reasonable fulfillment of past projects is accepted as sufficient. Future planning is complemented by pleasant reminiscing as the process of realizing life closure becomes more apparent. If delayed, this process can turn into frantic depression. If begun early enough, the process of life closure can be exhilarating. Remembering with pleasure life's labors and achievements should not be denied the aged. (Some gerontologist claim there must always be "a project," something to produce, else death sets in. This is nothing but the work ethic at its worst.) It is something else to encourage the imagination to go uncontrolled.

42

Reminiscing can encounter certain pitfalls and labor under false notions. Riley (1978) identified some of these to which can be added Henig's (1978) myth of senility.

Contrary to popular belief, most old people are not destitute, dependent, residing in nursing homes, seriously disabled and feeling inadequate. Work productivity does not decline in old age. Most are satisfied with their roles.

The life-course fallacy is taking a generalization from a cross-section of one age cohort and attributing it to the aging process itself. Mannheim (1952) had shown that each new cohort, starting its life at a unique point in history, has unique characteristics. Life has no single course to run.

"Age-reification" is the fallacy of assuming chronological age is a sausal factor in life (one becomes resigned because he is age fifty, according to Sheehy).

"Cohort-centrism" is the fallacy that members of the same age group share "a common location" in the social process. It is misleading to look for universals in the aging process at the expense of individual potential.

"Quantification" is a fallacy that governs thinking about aging all too often. Quantified data yields statements that are taken to be more dogmatic than the Pope; and they are as frequently misunderstood. Variables not originally included are attached to what most people do, as the normative influence of "hard facts" take hold of the imagination.

Senility is the most insidious form of ageism (Henig, 1978). Under its influence, older people give up their powers of life, either through their own misapprehensions or through social pressures equally affected by this misunderstanding. Senility is the main opponent of life course.

Life closure treated in this unit is theoretically lacking in certain practical or activist components

taken up in the final unit. Reflection on life closure
should not be done without them.

Unit 16. Religions in Service

Topics: Church-related programs. Nationwide
efforts. Seminary training. National centers and organizations.

In 1961 Barron reported that there was "very little
indication that organized religion had succeeded in
helping most of the aged adjust to their personal and
social situation" (p.161). Later, Hammond (1969) reported a surprisingly varied list of programs were to be
found, but that there was no clear theoretical basis
for evaluating them. Moberg (1978) reports that, ironi-
cally, church programs have systematically avoided the
role of religion in human well-being to protect religious liberty and separation of church and state. Yet,
Campbell (reported by Moberg) discovered that religious
faith is one of the significant domains giving people
a sense of well-being and satisfaction.

It is frequently heard (from public agencies as
well as the public generally) that the churches are do-
ing nothing for the aging and that the few programs
involve few people. That the federally funded programs
reach less than one per cent of the elderly in this
country is no excuse. But attention is being paid by
the churches on several levels and on several scales.

On the theoretical level, churches, such as the
U. S. Catholic Conference and the Lutheran Church of
America have already published action statements rela-
tive to the aging. So has the Synagogue Council of
America. Numerous pamphlets and handbooks are begin-
ning to appear, the most complete libraries for which
are those of the National Council on the Aging in
Washington, D. C. and, for the Midwest, the Mid-America
Resource and Training Center on Aging in Kansas City,
Missouri.

On a national scale there are ecclesiastical organizations such as the Catholic Charities, represented
also on the diocesan scale. The most frequently found
and perhaps the best is the ecumenical format in which

44

the local ministerial associations have coordinated
area programs in which the local churches and synagogues participate.

On the level of training in pastoral care,
seminaries such as St. Paul United Methodist Seminary
have established gerontology chairs. More often, however, one finds the introduction of single gerontology
courses into the seminary curriculum.

Among the oldest institutions of the church
is the religion-sponsored or religion-related nursing
homes. Methodist homes existed over and century and a
quarter ago. A Catholic order of Carmelite nuns was
founded with care of the elderly as its chief aposto-
late.

Perhaps the best model for local caring for
the elderly is the Shepherd's Center in Kansas City,
Missouri. It is inspired by Judeo-Christian values and
funded largely by area churches and synagogues. Religious bodies are represented on the governing board. It
is ecumenical in approach and freely uses the resources
of religious faith, without proselytizing, to cope with
changes, losses and challenges encountered in the aging
process.

In response to the many requests for advice
and assistance the Center established a resource and
training center on aging which conducts workshops in
the center and elsewhere. Library resources include
bibliographies (in twenty-six categories) and audio-
visual equipment (tapes, films, filmstrips, etc.).

The 1971 White House Conference on Aging; Spiritual Well-Being Section included among its recommendations encouraging religious organizations to meet
spiritual needs, to make religious consultation available and to evaluate program effectiveness upon the
spiritual well-being of the elderly.

One direct result of this Conference was the
establishment of the National Interfaith Coalition on
Aging, Inc. (NICA) in order to enable national level

church leadership to coordinate meaningful response
to problems of aging. Their newsletter, _Inform_, regularly circulates information about national, regional
and local programs.

A most interesting feature of these programs
is their sectarian-free attitude and ecumenical atmosphere. There is in this phenomenon something of a
loss of the uniqueness of each cooperating unit. At
this point, at least, there is little value in judging
this feature one way or the other.

Unit 17. Church and State in Cooperation

Topics: Practical, theoretical, legal and
religious issues.

Federal funding supports many church-related
programs. If the elderly were not so ignored by the
rest of society, much fuss would undoubtedly be raised.
The main issues in practice concern holistic service to
the elderly. The local churches and synagogues may conduct excellent meal programs, but, as Moberg (1978)
and others point out, precious little relates to personal fulfillment.

That greater cooperation between the religions
and the federal government is encouraged on both sides
leads to many theoretical issues. Up to this time, the
relationship was either a silent partnership (chaplaincies in the armed forces, prayer breakfasts, etc.) or
a strident conflict. Aging programs will raise many
of the questions about the relationship as well as a-
bout the role of religions in public life and the role
of the state in private life.

Legal challenges are bound to arise. It
seems obvious from some of the White House recommendations: Recommendation IV provides for federal funding
of some chaplaincies; V, for government evaluation of
the effectiveness of spiritual well-being programs;
and XII, for national policy for religious bodies to
function as providers of interfaith broad-based community programs.

Religious questions arising pertain to civil

religion, the nature of religious commitment, how it is validly quantified, the extent to which different religious groups can cooperate and many more.

Unit 18.   The New Generation

Topics: Fourth Generation. New Generation. Young-Old. Letting-go and picking-up: Social responsibility and authority.

Notice is being taken of a "fourth generation" (Morgan:1978), those whose number is growing, who live over 75 years. They serve to bring attention to the generation preceding them, the 55-75 roughly speaking. The needs of the fourth generation are basically the same as those of the third generation, of those who do not live to see the fourth. The new generation is the third, or perhaps the fourth, with Morgan's fourth as fifth.

In traditional societies, a person passed rather sharply from childhood, through a rite de passage into adulthood. In post-industrial societies, however, a distinctly different and unique stage of life asserted itself: that of the teenager, with rights, privileges and (few) obligations of its own. Psychology called it adolescence.

Today a new generation is being born at the other end of the age spectrum. One would be tempted to call it senescence, but this term is used in the biological process of deterioration, which leads Atchley (1977:37) to say "the skin of an older person is a considered a badge of inferiority." Surely ageist remarks such as this are in direct conflict with traditional respect for one's elders. Gutmann (cf. Unit 2) observed how the elder passed into a position of prestige and honor. Atchley is unfortunately speaking for modern society. Even worse, he is accurate. The counterpart in Hinduism is that of "retirement" and, in Buddhism, that of "compassion." They are between the very active middle-aged and very idle old-age individuals (Hapsgood: 1978). Neugarten (1978) finds this a relatively healthy group, better educated than any in the past, financially

47

secure and ready to become social contributors as well
as self-fulfilled.

At this phase in life, there is no career to
build at the expense of others. There is a realism
about life in which many unreleased projects are re-
leased from future planning. Youthful dreams are re-
interpreted in the light of individual and social conditions to "make the best of a good situation." Having
let lesser goals go, this generation will pick up on
more important and more meaningful enterprises.

The new generation comes to birth before retirement, in the time of pre-retirement, when the
individual takes stock of his or her future. Retirement is
a passage to a more free life.

Current sociologies of retirement could have
much to offer in understanding the possibilities, but
they are still struggling with the individual's adjustment to the day of retirement itself. It is interesting
that, while ancient societies, which respected their
elderly, had no appropriate rite of passage; modern
society, which is noted for its disrespect through
neglect of the elderly, has invented retirement rituals,
commonly known as the entry into the role of the role-
less (cf. Atchley: 1976). Cowgill (1972, 1974a and 1974b)
has documented the obvious (to many people at least):
standing of older people is lessened. Gutmann has noted
the same results among the Druze in the Middle East.
When MCRA states first among its aims:

> to appreciate the dignity of aging and to
> respect the unique authority which comes
> with aging in wisdom and knowledge (cf. "D"
> p.10. above),

it seeks to reverse these modern tendencies, or at least
to retard their ill effects.

The final step in the MCRA curriculum is to
invite the student to consider coming to terms with his
or her own aging. All that is said of the aged, may
one day be said of the younger set.

It is said of one of the saints that upon
seeing a drunk in the gutter, he exclaimed: "There
but for the grace of God, am I." Looking at an old
person--hopefully in better circumstances--he might
have exclaimed: "There <u>with</u> the grace of God, I will
be." Or, as the fearless 85-year old woman commented
on going about town: "They can even take my purse.
They can take anything. They can even take my life.
But no one can take away my eighty-one years."
Older persons have something the younger person does
and might never possess: a longer lifespan.

Having completed MCRA, the student is better
equipped to come to terms with his or her own aging.
MCRA has studiously avoided the temptation to play
the role of spiritual director to the student. Nevertheless, it should be clear that coming to terms with
one's own aging, or at least, seriously attempting to
do so, is a necessary prerequisite for anyone endeavor-
ing to implement goals and objectives in anyway similar
to those of MCRA.

PERIODICAL ABBREVIATIONS

AJO	AMERICAN JOURNAL OF ORTHOPSYCHIATRY
AM PSY	AMERICAN PSYCHOLOGIST
ARCH PSY	ARCHIVES OF PSYCHOLOGY
ASR	AMERICAN SOCIOLOGICAL REVIEW
CH	CHURCH HISTORY
CI ST	CHICAGO STUDIES
CHR CENT	CHRISTIAN CENTURY
COMM	COMMENTARY
CRIT	CRITIC
EG	EDUCATIONAL GERONTOLOGY
GER	THE GERONTOLOGIST
HPR	HOMILETIC AND PASTORAL REVIEW
HUM	THE HUMANIST
HUM DEV	HUMAN DEVELOPMENT
IJAHD	INTERNATIONAL JOURNAL OF AGING AND HUMAN DEVELOPMENT
IND J TH	INDIAN JOURNAL OF THEOLOGY
JAAR	JOURNAL OF THE AMERICAN ACADEMY OF RELIGION
JAGS	JOURNAL OF THE AMERICAN GERIATRIC SOCIETY
JCS	JOURNAL OF CHURCH AND STATE
JG	JOURNAL OF GERONTOLOGY
JGP	JOURNAL OF GERIATRIC PSYCHIATRY
JPC	JOURNAL OF PASTORAL CARE
JRH	JOURNAL OF RELIGION AND HEALTH
JSP	JOURNAL OF SOCIAL PSYCHOLOGY
LL	LIVING LIGHT
RE	RELIGIOUS EDUCATION
RV RLG	REVIEW FOR RELIGIOUS
RV REL RES	REVIEW OF RELIGIOUS RESEARCH
SC TH	SOCIAL THOUGHT
SF	SOCIAL FORCES
SOC AN	SOCIOLOGICAL ANALYSIS
SOC ED	SOCIAL EDUCATION
SWJTH	SOUTHWEST JOURNAL OF THEOLOGY
TD	THEOLOGY DIGEST

BIBLIOGRAPHY

1. RELIGIONS AND AGING: GENERAL

    a. MCRA*references not especially concerned with
       aging.

Berger, P. and T. Luckmann
    1963   "Sociology of Religion and Sociology of
              Knowledge," in R. Robertson, ed., Socio-
              logy of Religion. New York: Pelican, 1969,
              pp. 61-74.

Eliade, M.
    1954   Cosmos and History. Trans. W. Trask. Prince-
              ton, NJ: Princeton University Press.

Jacobsen, Thorkild
    1946   "Mesopotamia," in H. Frankfort, et al.,
              eds., Before Philosophy. Chicago: Univer-
              sity of Chicago Press.

Middleton, John
    1955   "The Concept of 'Bewitching' in Lugbara,"
              in John Middleton, ed., Magic, Witchcraft
              and Curing. New York: Natural History
              Press, pp. 54-67.

Marty, Martin
    1972   "Ethnicity: The Skeleton of Religion in
              America," CH 41:5-21.

Mascaro, Juan, trans.
    1965   The Upanishads. New York: Pelican Books.

Mc Kenzie, John L.
    1959   "Elders in the Old Testament." Biblica 40:
              522-540.

    1965   Dictionary of the Bible. Milwaukee: Bruce.

    1974   A Theology of the Old Testament. New York:
              Doubleday.

*A Model Curriculum On Religions and Aging

53

Richey, Russell E. and Donald G. Jones, eds.
    1974   American Civil Religion. New York: Harper
            Forum Books.

Sanders, N. K.
    1972   The Epic of Gilgamesh. Revised Edition
            Incorporating new material. New York:
            Penguin Books.

van Gennep, Arnold
    1960   The Rites of Passage. M. Vizedom and G.
            Caffee, trans. Chicago: The University
            of Chicago Press.

    b. Aging and Religion

Ansiello, E.F.
    1977   "Old Age and Literature: An Overview,"
            EG 2:211-218.

Baines, John
    1979   "Aging and World Order." The Whole Earth
            Papers. No. 13, Global Education Associates.

Biblin, Gratton C.
    1977   "Summaries of Selected Works on Aging
            Gracefully." Humanitas 13:127-133.

Bockle, F.
    1975   "Theological-ethical Aspects of Aging."
            TD 23:235-240.

Bradley, E.
    1976   "Growing Old Along With Me." Sisters
            Today 48:148-155.

Brubaker, T.H. and E.A. Powers
    1976   "The Sterotype of 'Old'--A Review and
            Alternative Approach." JG 31:441-447.

Bultena, Gorden and Edward A. Powers
    1978   "Denial of Aging: Age Identification and
            Reference Group Orientations. "JG 33:748-754.

54

Charles, D.C.
    1977   "Literary Old Age: A Browse Through
            History," EG 2:237-253.

Cohen, Stephen Z. and Bruce Michael Gans
    1978   The Other Generation Gap. Chicago:Follett.

Cowgill, Donald O.
    1972   "A Theory of Aging in Cros--Cultural
            Perspective." Donald O. Cowgill and L.
            Holmes, eds., Aging and Modernization.
            New York: Appleton-Century Crofts. Pp.
            1-14.

    1974a   "The Aging of Populations and Societies."
            F. Eisele, ed., Political Consequences of
            Aging. Philadelphia:American Academy of
            Political and Social Sciences. Pp 1-18.

    1974b   "Aging and Modernization: Revision of the
            Theory." J. Gubrium, ed. Communities and
            Environmental Policies. Pp. 123-146.

    1977   "The Revolution of Age." Hum 37; 5:10-13.

Creen, Edward and Henry Simmons
    1977   "Towards an Understanding of Religious
            Needs in Aging Persons." JPC 31:273-278.

Donohue, J.
    1978   "Unfair Shares: Discrimination Against
            Older Americans." America 138 (March 4)
            Pp. 170-172.

Fischer, E.
    1978   "Aging as Worship." Worship 52:98-108.

Flynn, Mary J.
    1977   Proceedings of the Working Conference on
            Pre-Retirement and Aging Among Clergy and
            Religious. Co-sponsored by: Center for the
            Study of Pre-Retirement and Aging, National
            Catholic School of Social Service, The
            Catholic University of America and Commis-
            sion on Aging, National Conference of Catho-
            lic Charities, Washington, D.C.

Fukuyama, Yoshio
    1962   "The Uses of Sociology: By Religious
            Bodies." JAAR 2:195-203.

Glock, C.Y.
    1962   "On the Study of Religious Commitment."
            RE 57 (Suppl) 98-110.

Gross, Ronald and Beatrice Gross and Sylvia Seidman
    1978   The New Old: Struggling for Decent Aging.
            New York: Anchor Press Doubleday.

Hapgood, David
    1978   "The Aging are Doing Better." The New Old:
            Struggling for Decent Aging. New York:
            Doubleday. pp. 345-363.

Henig, Robin M.
    1978   "Exposing the Myth of Aging." New York
            Times Magazine Section, December 3.

Hiltner, Seward, et al.
    1975   Towards a Theology of Aging. New York:
            Human Sciences Press. (A Special Issue of
            Pastoral Psychology 24:93-181.)

Howe, Reuel L.
    1980   "The Power of the Spirit in the Aging."
            Religion Journal of Kansas, Vol. 17, No.4.

John, Martha Tyler
    1977   "Teaching Children About Older Family
            Members." Soc.Ed. 41:524-527.

Knapp, M.R.J.
    1977   "The Activity Theory of Aging: An Examina-
            tion in the English Context." Ger.17:
            553-559.

LeFavre, Carol and Perry
    1981   Aging and the Human Spirit. Chicago:
            Exploration Press.

Mannheim, Karl
    1952   The Problem of Generations." Paul Kecske-
             meti, ed., Essays on the Sociology of
             Knowledge. London: Routledge and Kegan.
             Pp. 276-320.

Mindel, C.H.
    1975   "Multigenerational Family Living: A Viable
             Alternative for the Aged in Industrial
             Society." Paper read at the 10th Inter-
             national Congress of Gerontology, Jerusalem.

Moberg, David O.
    1965a   "Religion in Old Age." Geriatrics 20:977-982.

    1965b   "Religiosity in Old Age." Ger. 5:78-87.

    1967   "The Encounter of Scientific and Religious
             Values Pertinent to Man's Spiritual Nature."
             Soc.An. 25:22-23.

    1971   Spiritual Well-Being: Background and Issues.
             Washington, D.C.: 1971 White House Conference
             on Aging.

    1978   "Spiritual Well-Being and the Quality of
             Life Movement: A New Arena for Church-
             State Debate?" (Guest Editorial) JCS
             20:427-449.

    1974   "Spiritual Well-Being in Late Life." J.
             Gubrium, ed., Late Life: Communities and
             Environmental Policies. Pp. 256-279.

    1979b   Spiritual Well-Being: Sociological Perspec-
             tives. Washington, D.C.: University Press
             of America.

Morgan, John
    1978   The Fourth Generation. Minneapolis:
             Augsberg.

Monk, Abraham
    1977   "The Age of Aging." Hum 37:6-8.

Neugarten, B.L.
    1974   "Age Groups in American Society and the
            Rise of the Young-Old." Annals 415
            (September) Pp. 187-198.

    1975   "The Future of the Young-Old." Ger. ;5"4-9.

    1978   "The Rise of the Young-Old," in R. Gross,
            et al., eds., The New Old:Struggling for
            Decent Aging. New York: Doubleday. pp. 47-49.

Palmore, Erdman B.
    1974   "Modernization and the Status of the Aged:
            International Correlations." JG 29:205-210.

    1975   The Honorable Elders: A Cross-Cultural
            Analysis of Aging in Japan, Durham: Duke
            University Press.

    1976   "The Future Status of the Aged." Ger. 16:
            297-302.

Peterson, D.A.
    1976   "Aging in America in the Year 2000." JG
            16:264-270.

Riley, Matilda White
    1978   "Aging Social Change and the Power of
            Ideas," Daedalus 107:39-52.

Rogers, Tommy
    1976   "Manifestations of Religiosity and the
            Aging Process." RE 71:405-415.

Rose, A. and W. Peterson, eds.
    1965   Older People and their Social World.
            Philadelphia, PA: F.A. Davis, Co.

Stagg, Frank
    1981   The Bible Speaks on Aging. Broadman Press.

Stewry, S.
    1976   "The Later Years: A Psychological Perspec-
            tive." Soc. Th. 2:23-32.

Seefeldt., C., et al.
    1977   "Using Pictures to Explore Children's
            Attitudes Towards the Elderly," Ger. 17:
            506-512.

Storey, Denise C.
    1977   "Gray Power: An Endangered Species? Ageism
            as Portrayed in Children's Books," Soc.
            Ed. 41:528-530.

Stout, Robert J.
    1977   "Our Misfit Children, Young and Old."
            Chr. Cent. 94:194-196.

Streib, G.F. and C.J. Schneider
    1971   Retirement in American Society: Impact
            and Process. Ithaca, NY: Cornell Univer-
            sity Press.

Urbach, E.E.
    1971   "The Talmudic Sage - Character and Autho-
            rity," Jewish Society Through the Ages
            (ed., H.H. Ben Sasson and S. Ettinger).
            New York: Schocken. Pp. 117-147

van Tassel, David D., ed.
    1979   Aging, Death and the Completion of Being.
            Philadelphia: University of Pennsylvania
            Press.

Wolff, Hans Walter
    1974   "To Be Young and To Grow Old," in Anthro-
            pology of the Old Testament. Philadelphia:
            Fortress. pp. 119-127.

2. RELIGION AND DISENGAGEMENT

Bahr.
    1970   "Aging and Religious Disaffiliation." SF
            49:59-71.

Cath, S.H.
    1975   "The Orchestration of Disengagement,"
            IJAHD 6:199-213.

Clemente, E., P.A. Rexford and C. Hirsch
    1975   "The Participation of the Black Aged in
            Voluntary Associations." JG 30:469-472.

Cook, John W.
    1975   "Application of the Disengagement Theory
            of Aging to Elderly Persons in the Church,"
            RE 70:438.

Cumming, Elaine and W. Henry
    1981   Growing Old: The Process of Disengagement.
            New York: Basic Books.

Cutler, S.J.
    1977   "Aging and Voluntary Association Partici-
            pation," JG 32:470-479.

Hochschild, A.
    1975   "Disengagement Theory: A Critique and a
            Proposal," ASR 40:553-569.

Laniers, C.E.
    1975   "Perceptions of Aging Parents in the Con-
            text of Disengagement Theory." Genetic
            Psychology Monograph 92.

Lazerwitz, B.
    1962   "Memberships in Voluntary Associations and
            Frequency of Church Attendance." JAAR 2"
            74-84.

May, William F.
    1976   "Institutions as Symbols of Death." JAAR
            44:212-223.

Moberg, David O.
  1953a   "Church Membership and Personal Adjust-
           ment in Old Age." JG 8:207-211.

  1953b   "Leadership in the Church and Personal
           Adjustment in Old Age." Sociol. Soc. Res.
           37:312-316.

  1965a   "Religiosity in Old Age." Ger. 5:78-87.

  1965b   "Church Participation and Adjustment in
           Old Age." in A.M. Rose and W.A. Peterson,
           eds., Older People and Their Social World
           The Subculture of the Aging. Philadelphia:
           Davis.

Mindel, C. and E.C. Vaughan
  1978   "A Multidimensional Approach to Religiosity
           and Disengagement." JG 33:103-108.

3. LIFE SATISFACTION AND LIFE REVIEW

Atchley, R.C.
    1971   "The Leisure of the Elderly." Hum. 5:14-16.

    1976   The Sociology of Retirement. New York:
            John Wiley & Sons.

Barrett, W.
    1976   "On Returning to Religion." Comm. 62,5:
            33-47.

Bell, B.D.
    1974   "Cognitive Dissonance and the Life Satis-
            faction of Older Adults." JG 29:564-571.

Borges, M.A. and L.J. Dutton
    1976   "Attitudes toward Aging: Increasing Op-
            timism found with Age." JG 16:220-224.

Boykin, L.S.
    1975   "Soul Foods for Some Older Americans."
            JAGS 23:380-382.

Boylin, W., S.K. Gordon and M.F. Merle
    1976   "Reminiscing and Ego Integrity in Insti-
            tutional Elderly Males.: JG 16:118-124.

Braceland, F.
    1977   "Personal Reflections on Growing Olders."
            Crit. 35:66-68.

Bull, C.
    1975   "Voluntary Association, Participation and
            Life Satisfaction." JG 40:73-76.

Bultena, Gordon and Edward A. Powers
    1978   "Denial of Aging: Age Identification and
            Reference Group Orientations." JG 33:
            748-754.

Butler, R.M.
    1974   "Successful Aging and the Role of Life
            Review." JAGS 22:529-599.

Carp, F.M.
    1975   "Impact of Improved Housing on Morale and Life Satisfaction." Ger. 15:511-515.

Chatfield, W.F.
    1977   "Economic and Sociological Factors Influencing Life Satisfaction of the Aged." JG 32:593-599.

Committee on Psychiatry and Religion
    1976   Mysticism: Spiritual Quest or Psychic Disorder. Publication No. 97:703-823.

Covalt, N.K.
    1958   "The Meaning of Religion to Older People: A Medical Perspective." in D.L. Scheder, ed., Organized Religion and the Older Person. Gainesville: University of Florida Press. Pp. 78-90.

    1960   "The Meaning of Religion to Older People." Geriatrics 15: 658-664.

Cowgill, Donald O.
    1976   "A Previous Incarnation of Disengagement Theory: An Historical Note." Ger. 16:377-378.

Cunningham, A.
    1976   "Finding a Continuing Meaning to Life." Chi.St. 15: 139-147.

Dowd, J.J.
    1975   "Aging as Exchange: A Preface to Theory." JG 30:584-594.

Edwards, John E.
    1973   "Correlate of Life Satisfactions: A Re-examination." JG 28: 497-502.

Flanagan, John C.
    1978   "A Research Approach to Improving our Quality of Life." Am. Psy. 33:138-147.

Fontana, A.
1977   The Last Frontier: The Social Meaning of
        Growing Old. Beverly Hills: Sage Publica-
        tions.

Gaffney, Sister Marie
1974   Growing Old. Chicago: Claretian Publications.

Giambra, L.M.
1977   "Daydreaming about the Past: The Time
        Setting of Spontaneous Through Intrusions."
        Ger. 17:35-38.

Graney, Marshall J.
1975   "Happiness and Social Participation in
        Aging." JG 30:701-706.

Harter, W.
1975   "Retirement: Your Age of Discovery." Li-
        guorian 63:40-48.

Hashien, L.
1976   "More Years or More Life." Soc. Th. 2:
        43-55.

Hehnek, A.
1977   "Continuity of Life Situation and Success-
        ful Aging." Aktuelle Gerontologie 7:301-304.

Henretta, J.C. and R.T. Campbell
1976   "Status Attainment and Status Maintenance:
        A Study of Stratification in Old Age." ASR
        41: 981-992.

Hiltner, Seward
1975   Toward a Theology of Aging. New York: Human
        Sciences Press.

Kavanough, M.
1975   "The Aging Relative's Right to Dignity."
        Marriage 57 (October), Pp. 18-20.

Keefe, T.
    1975   "Meditation and the Psychotherapist."
            AJO 45:484-489.

Kilduff, Thomas
    1980   "Aging" Spiritual Life. Washington, D.C.
            Washington Province of the Discalced Car-
            melite Fathers, Inc.. Vol. 26:3-20

Kirkendall, Lester
    1977   "Fulfillment in the Later Years." Hum.
            37,5:31-33.

Larson, R.
    1978   "Thirty Years of Research on the Subjective
            Well-Being of Older Americans." JG 33:
            109-125.

Lebowitz, B.D.
    1975   "Age and Fearfulness: Personal and Situ-
            ational Factors." JG 30:696-700.

Lohmann, Nancy L.
    1977   Comparison of Life Satisfaction, Morale
            and Adjustment Scales on an Elderly Pop-
            ulation. Ph.D.Diss. Brandeis.

Markson, Elizabeth W.
    1973   "The Elderly and the Community: Reidentify-
            ing Unmet Needs." JG 28:505-509.

McTavish, D.G.
    1971   "Perception of Old People: A Review of
            Research Methodologies and Findings."
            Gerontologist 11:90-101.

Michenbaum, D.
    1974   "Self-instructional Strategy Training: A
            Cognitive Prosthesis for the Aged." Hum.
            Dev. 17:273-281.

Miserve, Harry C.
    1976   "Second Life," (Editorial) JRH 15,6:3-6.

Moberg, David O.
  1951   Religion and Personal Adjustment in Old
            Age. Ph. D.Diss. University of Minnesota.

  1956   "Religious Activities and Personal Adjust-
            ment in Old Age." JSP 43:261-267.

  1971   "Spiritual Well-Being: Background and Issues."
            White House Conference on Aging, Washington,
            D.C.

  1979a   "Spiritual Well-Being and the Quality of
            Life Movement: A New Arena for Church-
            State Debate?" Journal of Church and
            State 20:427-449.

  1980   Developments and Issues Related to Spiri-
            tual Well-Being and Ethical Concerns in
            Aging since the 1971 White House Conference.
            Erlanger, Kentucky.

Nouwen, Henri and Walter J. Gaffney
  1976   Aging: The Fulfillment of Life. New York:
            Doubleday.

Rowe, A.R.
  1976   "Retired Academics and Research Activity."
            JG 31:456-461.

Stagg, Frank
  1981   The Bible Speaks on Aging. Broadman Press.

Stickle, F.
  1977   "Satisfying the Emotional Needs of the
            Elderly: A Call for Counselors." Council
            and Values 21:180-184.

Swartz, Eleanor
  1978   "The Older Adult: Creative Use of Leisure
            Time." JGP 11:85-87.

Thorson, J. and T.C. Cook, eds.
  1977   Spiritual Well-Being and the Elderly.
            Springfield, MO.: Charles Thomas Publishers.

Thraven, Eleanor L.
    1977   Life Satisfaction of the Aged: A Recon-
            ceptualization of the Measurement Crite-
            ria. Ph. D.Diss. Brandeis.

Ward, R.A.
    1977   "The Impact of Subjective Age and Stigma
            of Older Persons." JG 32:227-232.

Wimmer, Donald H.
    1982   "Aging and Wisdom: East & West." Religion
            Journal of Kansas, Vol. 19, No. 2,
            January, 1982.

4. RELIGIONS IN SERVICE

Anderson, Ruth E.
1977   Library Resources. Mid-America Resource
        and Training Center on Aging (Kansas City,
        MO.).

1979   Audio Visual Catalog Addendum. Mid-America
        Resource and Training Center (Kansas City,
        MO.).

Ankenbrandt, T.
1976   "The Church and Mature Christians: Reflec-
        tions on Pastoral Care fro the Elderly."
        America 135, 13:318-319.

Biwas, S.K.
1976   "Trends in the Church's Involvement in
        Social Service in the Past Twenty-Five
        Years." Ind.J.Th. 25:167-171

Brink, T.L.
1977   "Pastoral Care for the Aged: A Practical
        Guide." JPC 31:264-272.

Clements, William M., ed.
1981   Ministry with the Aging: Designs, Challenges,
        Foundations. San Francisco: Harper & Row.

Clingan, Donald F.
1975   Aging Persons in the Community of Faith.
        A Guidebook for Churches and Synagogues
        on Ministry to, for and with the Aging.
        Published for the Institute on Religion
        and Aging by the Indiana Commission on the
        Aging and the Aged. St. Louis: Christian
        Board of Education.

Cook, T.C., Jr. and McGinty, D.L. and Ziegler, J., eds.
1980   "Education for Ministry in Aging: Geron-
        tology in Seminary Training." Theological
        Education.

68

Covetelly, J.
    1976   "The Apostolate to Senior Parishioners."
            HPR 77:10-23.

Foley, J.
    1975   "Old Age for Religious: A Time of Aposto-
            lic Fruitfulness." Rv. Rel. 34:108-112.

Gallagher, Rt. Rev. Msgr. R. J.
    1964   "The Role of Religion in Assisting the
            Older Individual in Maintaining his Identi-
            ty and Well-Being in an Automated Society."
            Unpublished paper. National Council on
            the Aging Annual Meeeting, Chicago. Cf.
            NCOA, Washington, D.C.

Gray, R.M. and D.O. Moberg
    1962   The Church and the Older Person. Grand
            Rapids: Berdmans.

Hammond, Phillip E.
    1969   "Aging and the Ministry." Matilda W. Riley
            ed., in Aging and Society, Vol. 2 New
            York: Russell Sage Foundation. Pp. 293-323.

Hubbard, Richard
    1979   "Pastoral Care in the Nursing Home: Guide-
            lines for Communication with Institution-
            alized Elderly." Journal of Pastoral Care,
            Vol. XXXIII, No. 4. Pp. 239-242.

Keith, Pat M.
    1977   "Perceptions of the Needs of the Aged by
            Ministers and the Elderly." Rv. Rel. Res.
            18:278-282.

Longino, C.F., et..al.
    1976   "Parish Clergy and the Aged: Examining
            Sterotypes." JG 31:340-345.

Madden, D.
    1977   "Senior Road Runners: A Parish Program
            for Golden Agers.: Today's Parish 9:16-17.

Maves, P.B.
1960   "Aging, Religion and the Church." in C.
Tibbitts,ed., Handbook of Social Gerontology. Chicago: University of Chicago
Press. P$_p$. 698-749

National Council on Aging   (NCOA)
1976   Church Programs. (A bibliography from the
card catalog). Washington, D.C.: NCOA.

National Interfaith Coalition on Aging
1975   Spiritual Well-Being: A Definition and
Commentary. Athens, GA.

Peacock, Richard L.
1975   "Older Adult: The Church's Opportunity."
SWJTh 17:48-57.

Peralta, Vicky
1980   "Challenge of Aging and the Church." New
Catholic World. Vol. 223, No. 1335. Paulist
Press. P$_p$. 105-108.

Reichert, Sara and Richard Reichert
1976   In Wisdom and the Spirit: A Religious Education Program for Those Over Sixty-Five.
New York: Paulist Press.

Rhode Island Council of Churches
1980   Suggested Guidelines for Nursing Home
Ministry. Providence, Rhode Island.

Shapero, Sanford M.
1975   "Vintage Years: General View and Jewish
Challenge." JRH 14:120-141.

Synagogue Council in America
1975   That Thy Days May Be Good In The Good
Land: A Guide To Aging Programs For
Synagogues. New York: Synagogue Council
of America.

70

van Wagner, Charles A.
    1977   "Supervision of Lay Pastoral Care." <u>JPC</u>
             31:158-163

Vincentia, Joseph, Sr.
    1977   "The Parish and Ministry to the Aging."
             <u>LL</u> 14:69-83

Appendix

AGING AND WISDOM: EAST AND WEST

By

Donald H. Wimmer

(Reprinted from Religion Journal of Kansas, Vol. 19,
No. 2, January, 1982.)

It may be surprising to some to learn that
one of the world's greatest religious traditions,
Buddhism, began with a series of experiences: old age,
sickness and death. The first was prompted by seeing
an old man.

This experience itself was nothing unusual.
The response to it was. A great religious tradition
sprang out of it because many people could identify
with the founder's experience with old age and the response he gave to it.

In addition to the experience of old age were
those of sickness and death. Death was experienced in
a negative way and then in a positive way. The experiences of sickness and "negative" death are essentially
the same as that of old age. They are experiences of
life limitation. Of these experiences, it is the
experience of old age that offers hope. Sickness has
something in common with old age: The experience of
physical helplessness which culminates in physical
death.

The experience of old age is not the same as
old age itself. The experience can come early or late
in life. Old age as an experience is a realization
that life for the most part has been lived and that the
major part that remains is that of life completion. It
prompts the willingness to do that which will bring a
sense of life completion.

Life completion evolves out of a sense of
the meaningfulness of life. It is an existential
answer to the question of what life is all about. The

73

Hindu prince, Siddhartha Gautama of the Sakyas, centuries ago saw an old man. What he saw was his own future. For all the privileges that royalty could confer on him, old age would crown them all. When Siddhartha saw a sick man, he saw that frailty does not necessarily wait until chronological age is advanced. Sickness anticipates the debilitating effects of advanced aging. What he must do to satisfy his desire to live must be done in advance of old age; it should be done early - before sickness jumps in ahead of time and renders life unable to accomplish anything except a miserable resignation.

Then Siddhartha saw a dead man. He saw a completed life. Did he saw unfulfilled dreams and frustrated desires? Or did he see satisfaction and completion? I think not. What he saw left him all questions and no answers.

Then Siddhartha saw a person who was in a sense both living and dead: living in the sense that the man had not yet died biologically; dead in the sense that the man had in a way completed his life. His lifestyle tolerated no ambitiousness. What Siddhartha saw was a monk.

A monk is a man who gives up his life to find a new life. He takes his whole life in hand and, in his intentions, disposes of the whole of it by assigning it to the goals of the monastic life. The remainder of his days is but a living-out of the whole-life decision. There is a sense of life completion in the taking of the vows. It is a completion that is further enlarged and fulfilled as each day goes by. Each day is lived as a gift over and above the life completed before becoming a monk.

What Siddhartha saw made a deep impression. His experience of old age culminated in a decision to take his whole life in hand, to do what the monks do. They had the secret of life, the wisdom of the ages. He would not need to live forever in unending pleasures of youth and royalty. At this moment, Siddhartha came of age. He left home to join the monks. In living their spiritual death he entered the continuum of satisfied life. The wisdom Siddhartha acquired enabled him

to make a mature life decision. His experience of a-
nother's old age rendered him "of age". If he does
what he wants to do, he should be able to die satisfied.
Moral of the story: Learn from the experiences of o-
thers. Anticipate the challenges brought by the frail-
ties of advanced aging before the challenges turn into
frustrations about life itself. This is conventional
wisdom. A word to the wise suffices - perhaps.

DEEPER THAN CONVENTIONAL WISDOM

But the story is not over; Siddhartha was not
enlightened by these experiences. The conventional wisdom did not work. It almost killed him. He adopted
such extreme austerities that his physical frame could
not cope with the results. Near biological death, he
left the woods and the monks, the whole bit.

In this moment, Siddhartha, frustrated, pressed
on. He was determined to find the key to life, that
instrument that would give life its meaning by unlocking
the door to the insight. He was determined to find it.
He pledged not to budge until he found it. Time would
stand still. Indeed, without meaning, time stood still,
or it crushed relentlessly and mercilessly on, killing
life minute by minute. To Siddhartha, it was "Do or
die!"

What did he do? He sat down under the nearest
tree, determined not to budge until he found the key to
life. He sought enlightenment.

What passed through his mind is anyone's
guess. His thoughts had to come from his experience.
He may have thought about what it means to be a Hindu.

Being a Hindu meant having the whole way of
life laid out for him to follow. It meant passing
through clearly delineated stages in life, using perhaps several yogas in pursuit of several wants or needs
and all of this as a member of one of the four castes.
His caste used to be that of the warrior, but ever
since the territories had been conquered, it was a
caste of administrators protecting and managing their
turf. As a prince he would have succeeded his father,
their king. This lost its appeal when he left home.

75

Siddhartha wanted enlightenment. He had
pursued the paths of desire at home, both the path of
immediate satisfaction (kama) and the path of planned
pleasure, artha, the pursuit of wealth, fame and power,
all of which were guaranteed to the future king. He
had also followed the path of extreme renunciation and
found it wanting. Left to him was dharma, the path of
community service, which offers a sort of fulfillment
in the service of others. He would have enjoyed the
wealth, good name and social influence needed to do
great, good things. Obviously, that did not appeal
to him or he would have returned home to take up where
he left off. In a way, he had already passed that
point in his life. By retiring to the woods with the
monks, he anticipated the standard, highly-valued stage
in Hindu life: retirement.

If, in his mystical experiences with the
monks, he had been transported somehow to modern America, he would at least have been happy to avoid that
bankruptcy of spirit that afflicts the retired producer
whose life-meaning evaporates the moment he leaves the
production line. Hindus at least honor and respect
their elders. Hindu society bestows upon the retired
person the dignity of living without a worker's mask.
A retired person can have a life-philosophy because,
first of all, he or she has lived a nearly completed
life. Desires either have been fulfilled or they have
been reviewed and adjusted. Those desires that cut into life and destroy its fullness, those that tear one
apart within one's own little world, are rejected. The
monk's way is one of seeing through maya, illusions of
non-life offered under the guise of life.

With the monks, Siddartha sought Brahman, true
reality. Retirement was not isolation and loneliness,
but a project of becoming one with "that which is."
He sought veda, true knowledge, which according to the
scriptures, underlies the superficialities of life and
social customs. At the same time he sought his true
self (atman). He sought "the Beyond that is within."
He pushed himself further than his body could handle
until he realized the monk's way did not possess the
key to enlightenment. So he left it behind, and, as he

sat under the Bo tree, he must have mulled over and
over again these and other teachings of the scriptures.

Finally, enlightenment came. Siddhartha became
the Enlightened One, the Buddha. Buddha then preached
the Deer Park Sermon in which he disclosed the Four
Noble Truths of Enlightenment. To him, all life is
dukkha, out-of-focus, disjointed. What it really means
is that the secret he sought does not exist. He wanted
the key which would open the door to a new vision of
life, one in which all the pieces would fall into place.
The truth is: There is none, so none can be expected--
at any age. The truly wise old man is one who knows
this. Buddha also knows what causes this disjointedness and how to eliminate it. The Enlightened Buddha
has achieved the True Wisdom of old age in the Four
Noble Truths: 1) Life is dukkha, disjointedness; 2)
Dukkha is caused by Trishna,desire; 3) to eliminate
Dukkha, disjointedness (or suffering) one has to eliminate Trishna, desire; and finally to eliminate Desire,
one has to follow the Eightfold Path.

To make a long story short on following the Eightfold Path, suffice it to say that the elimination of
desires culminates in the elimination of, in the very
last step, the desire to get rid of desires! As life
progresses, some desires are eliminated by being fulfilled. They then lead to greater desires. The attainment of some wealth, fame or power leads to the desire
to attain greater wealth, fame and power. These desires
can be overwhelming and misleading. This is false progress. They occupy us with things, not reality. Reality
is being a part of life, not being cut off from others.
Buddha teaches people to get rid of desires that cause
life to be disjointed. We can then be in touch with
life. This is true progress, true wisdom, which comes
all too often late in life. Wisdom comes with experience, and experience comes with age.

MESSAGE OF BUDDHISM

In his wisdom, Buddha is realistic about aging.
Advanced age means life is near completion. Desires
that are not yet fulfilled can be frustrating. To con-
tinue to entertain unattainable desires is to frustrate

life. On the other hand, a fulfilled life is one in
which no desires are frustrated. There comes a time
in life when the road to life fulfillment and life
completion passes through a process of rejecting
desires. The Noble Truths of Buddhism anticipate fulfillment, not in following the Hindu paths of desire
but in following the path of no-desires of Buddha, For
an old person who rejects desires that are frustrating
and useless, life continues with a sense of completion
and fulfillment. A wise person knows that one does
not have to wait for age to advance chronologically.
The enlightenment of the Buddha was an anticipation
of the wisdom of old age: The wisdom of learing how
to handle one's own desires.

To learn to master one's desires is to pursue the
wisdom of the East. To a certain extent it is also part
of the wisdom of the ancient Near East and of the Bible
as well. This can be illustrated in one way from the
Epic of Gilgamesh and in another from Ecclesiastes.

THE MESOPOTAMIAN TRADITION

The Epic of Gilgamesh[1] is the world's oldest ex-
tant epic. Parts of it date from the Early Bronze Age,
originating as it does in ancient Sumer in Mesopotamia
five millenia ago. It appears at a time when cuneiform
recorded literature in the best sense of the word, literature which embodied the values of even more ancient times
and preserved them for centuries upon centures later.
The Epic influenced thousands of years of human experience.
The experience it expresses and the values it conveys
are easily shared by everyone by identifying with the
hero, Gilgamesh.

At one point in the story, Gilgamesh, king of Uruk,
has experienced the death of his friend Enkidu. So
intensely does this force gilgamesh to realize that his
own limitations are unavoidable that he leaves Uruk in
search of the secret of life.

Scholars usually refer to this as a quest for immortality, but that concept is an abstraction and a
rather medieval notion. The concept of immortality does
not relate directly to the experience of the ancients.

78

The experience of life here and now does relate very
well. We must remember also the Gilgamesh is not just
an individual. He is king. He is responsible for the
future of Uruk. The secret of life is not immortality
as such. It is that which fulfills the desire to live.
For Gilgamesh it is at first the perpetual avoidance of
old age not only for himself but also for elders of
Uruk.

As the plot unravels, Gilgamesh learns that a
plant holds the secret of life. He must obtain it.
After the hero has surmounted the insurmountable, he
grasps the plant in his hand and heads for Uruk. (Were
he seeking immortality he would have eaten it and automatically achieved unending life. But that is not the
story.) Gilgamesh, sets out for Uruk with the plant
to give it to the elders there so that the old men may
eat of it and thereby be young again. Not that they
would become immature again, young and foolish, but
that they might implement the wisdom of their years
with youthful vim and vigor. But such is not to be.
Gilgamesh, wearied and thirsty, comes upon a pool.
Releasing the plant he puts it down at the edge of the
water and proceeds to refresh himself. At that moment
a serpent emerges from the water, steals the plant and
plunges back into the water to follow its deepest
channels far far away. Gilgamesh crestfallen, has to
return to Uruk empty-handed. The hero must accept the
limitations placed upon mankind by the gods. The point
is that if there ever was a way to avoid limiting life,
there is none any longer. The experience of aging is
an experience of increasing limitations that impose
themselves upon individuals without respect to royalty.
In this manner Gilgamesh parallels Siddhartha at the
moment of his first sight of an old man. The experience
for both men was quite valid. It changed their lives.
It offered insight into the true meaning of life.

Those who heard of the experiences of these men
and shared their insights believed the heroes' responses
were appropriate for people generally. The art of living
is learned by taking from these and other experiences
those humane values that contribute to life. Learning
from the experiences of others is education. Education
is the pursuit of wisdom. Learning from the experiences
of others is done consciously.

The experiences of Gilgamesh are conveyed in epic proportions so that the values they contain can be more readily recognized and more easily shared by storyteller and listener alike. The epic becomes part and parcel of the common experience or tradition of Mesopotamia. As such it is part of the foundation of later conventional wisdom. We know, for example, that parts of the epic were found in ancient Israel. A fragment of the flood story, which had become part of the epic of Gilgamesh by the time of the Old Testament, was found in Palestine from about the same time. The Mesopotamian experience is caught up in the Israelite experience and transformed by it.

THE WISDOM OF ANCIENT ISRAEL

Generally speaking, conventional wisdom is international, although each locale gives it its own peculiar qualities. In the case of ancient Israel the specific difference was a very important one; monotheism, the experience of the one and only God, as the Book of Genesis illustrates.

The experience reveals new dimensions to human living, some of them good, some not so good. The not-so-good is traditionally called "sin." Sinful human beings have chosen foolishly, and the Bible does not hesitate to "tell it like it is." The third chapter of Genesis depicts this feature of humanity: the foolishness that lies at the root of all subsequent human evil. The story of the Fall is presented as a wisdom narrative. It begins with the serpent being described as the wisest of all the creatures God had created. All the serpent does is to project a god other than the one who had revealed himself in his dialogue with Eve. The serpent plies Eve with false wisdom and the result is that she chooses foolishly: she chooses to ignore the self-revelation of the Lord.

She chooses to reject the knowledge that served as the basis for communication with her Maker and injects alienation into human community as well. When she takes the fruit she shares it. After all, sharing is what the first couple did best. Alienation characterizes the relationship between brothers, between families (Lamech) and nations (Babel). She, who took the fruit because it was beautiful to behold and "was useful in obtaining wisdom," foolishly set evil in motion. So the Yahwist tells us in the Hebrew Scriptures.

When the Priestly Writer edits earlier sources, he introduces his own theme to illustrate the results of this foolishness: decreasing lifespans. In round numbers, atediluvian patriarchs live many hundreds of years. After the flood, patriarchs live only several hundred years. Abraham, Issac and Jacob susequently live between one and two hundred years. Later generations have an even shorter lifespan. Shorter lifespans are the resultof foolish choices.

Nevertheless, subjectively speaking, the Israelite patriarchs die "full of days." To be old is to be blessed. "Full of days" means a complete life. The book of Proverbs honors old age: "The beauty of old men is their gray hair" (20:29). So does Sirach: "Whoever is wise will stay with the elders and listen to them" (6:34). "Rich experience is the crown of the aged and their boast is the fear of the Lord" (25:6). The fool on the other hand, "does not respect the gray hairs of the aged," according to the Wisdom of Solomon. Needless to say, the wise succeed while the fools fail. This is conventional wisdom.

Ecclesiastes criticizes this conventional wisdom. "Traditional wisdom often exhibited a shallow optimism and a too facile belief that virtue is always rewarded and wickedness always punished."[2]

According to traditional wisdom, youth by definition are those who do not have life experience. They are young and foolis-. The older one becomes, the wiser that person should be. That is why "there is no fool like an old fool." Traditional wisdom dictates that a person who wishes to fulfill the desire to live must find out what is needed to fulfill this desire and disregard all else as extraneous.

Any respectable search for the answer to the question of one's life proceeds from some kind of review of options and possibilities. Life review begins with an awareness of the aims and goals a person has

been pursuing. One is not bound by them. In fact, the
time for review is a time for modifying and implementing them, or for adopting new ones. It is a time to
decide to put an end to desires which are no longer
worth pursuing.

Once life goals are clarified and affirmed the
strategy for attaining them can be designed. This is
the step of finding out more precisely what it is that
can or must be done to fulfill the desire to live. This
step usually tends to simplify matters by giving them
perspective which, in turn, lends life a sense of
integration and a hope for completion.[3]

Traditional or conventional wisdom duly observed
should lead when all is in order, to life satisfaction.
At that moment life experience becomes one of fullness,
even though life is not completed biologically or
chronologically. Indeed, if the aims and goals are not
too ambitious, if they are basically completed the
sense of completion imbues every further phase of life
with an enjoyment that prevails over anxieties. A
special satisfaction comes from the realization that
pleasures over and above what is needed to fulfill
requirements for life satisfaction are additional gifts.
Those who desire more are gifted less. Moreover, they
are more prone to disappointment and frustration.

Retirement is the reward of a well-spent life,
according to conventional wisdom. The fool on the
other hand, earning no retirement, has made no provisions for old age. In this day and age the wise are
often made fools because society deprives them of digni-
fied retirement. Traditional wisdom based on conventional perceptions of justice breaks down frequently. "Good
guys finish last."

Ecclesiastes has something to say about this
situation. The author must have been not only very
wise, but also very old, on the verge of extreme old age.
His words of wisdom concern the use of wisdom itself
and the status of conventional wisdom in the eyes of
the exceedingly old. People listen to conventional
wisdom very simplistically. Wisdom should work like

the gimmicks crafty people use to get ahead. Not so
for Ecclesiastes; wisdom should be employed wisely,
not mechanically.

The wisdom of Ecclesiastes addresses many issues.
The final chapters of his collection deal with the
facts of extreme old age; loneliness and isolation.
Those days are evil days (12:1), when the once strong
are bent with age. They stay inside with doors locked,
while through the window they watch the world go by.
Loss of hearing reduces the sound of the mill. It
deprives them of the chirp of the bird and the song
of the maiden. Loss of sight and physical agility
make them fear heights and the perils of the street
(12:3-5). All these things show how the peripheries
of life are closing in on them. Isolation and loneliness replace the alleged values of wisdom, pleasure,
work, wealth and power. None of these offer life the
satisfaction it deserves. The time of gray hair, "when
the almond tree blossoms," becomes the time when the
locust grows sluggish and the caperberry (appetite
stimulant) loses its effect.

ACCEPTANCE AND ENJOYMENT

Extreme old age is the preamble to death, according to Ecclesiastes. It is the time the silver cord
is snapped, when one's pitcher is symbolically broken
and the breath of life from God returns to him (12:6-7).
Extreme old age is a time of darkness. Says Ecclesiastes
accept this and deal with it. "However, many years
a man may live, as he enjoys them all, remember that
the days of darkness are many. All that is to come
is vanity, (empty of substance)" (12:8).

To say that all days are to be enjoyed suggests
that the days of darkness are not meant to be without
some kind of satisfaction. Darkness refers to physical debilities and limitations and to the loneliness
and isolation that can accompany old age. If one is
not deceived by myths of senility[4] and discouraged by
the loss of physical mobility, spiritual well-being
has a chance. The power of the spirit can move an
otherwise lethargic body--but only to a point. The
human spirit is not inexhaustible. Although Ecclesiates'
wisdom about traditional wisdom enables people to pass

83

Beyond the normal cycles of prosperity and success
when the loss of physical well-being is not accom-
panied by the loss of spirit, he frequently reminds
us that no human system is capable of providing a
panacea. As it would for Gilgamesh, setting forth on
his journey, traditional wisdom would propose to us to
have something unique, enduring and definitvely satisfying. But it cannot provide a basis for living. It
is not the key to life. Life is disjointed. Buddha
is right. Not even recollecting a fulfilled life can
give complete, total and permanent satisfaction. "The
profundity of Ecclesiastes is its perception of the
total inability of man to work out enduring happiness
by his own resources...Ecclesiastes believes that God
grants man a certain portion of pleasure in a normal
life and toil spent to acquire more than his portion
is vanity and pursuit of the wind."[5] He would agree
with Job that only experience of God can enable sufficient insight into life to give it coherence and meaning. Not even the experience of God removes the darkness of old age. It enables one to live with it.

     Remember your Maker in the days of your youth,
before the evil days come, and the years draw nigh.
when you will say, "I have no pleasure in them."
advises Ecclesiastes. The Creator has put it all together and the cycles of nature will run their appoint-
ed courses. Man is not the master of the cosmos. God
is. God grants a modest portion of life and pleasure
to each person who should accept it gratefully for
what it is. In other words, his advice to the wise is
for them to be somewhat detached from their life goals
and relaxed about the key strategies they have designed
for the purposes of achieving life satisfaction. It is
faith in God that enables a person to deal even-handed
with personal desires and to know that

"For everything ther is a season
and a time for every activity under heaven:

          A time to be born
                    and a time to die;
          a time to plant
                    and a time to uproot;
          a time to kill
                    and a time to heal;

```
        a time to pull down
                        and a time to build up;
        a time to weep
                        and a time to laugh;
        a time to mourn
                        and a time to dance;
        a time to scatter stones
                        and a time to gather them;
        a time to embrace
                and a time to refrain from embracing;
        a time to seek
                        and a time to lose
        a time to keep
                        and a time to throw away;
        a time to tear
                        and a time to mend;
        a time to keep silence
                        and a time to speak;
        a time to love
                        and a time to hate;
        a time for war
                        and a time for peace."
```

                                        (Ecclesiastes 3)

Notes

1. The Epic of Gilgamesh, translated by N.K. Sanders.
    Revised edition with new material (New York: Pen-
    guin, 1972).

2. John L. Mc Kenzie, "Ecclesiastes," Dictionary of
    the Bible (New York: Macmillan, 1965).

3. See Erik Erikson, Childhood and Society (New York:
    W.W. Norton & Company, 1963) and David O. Moberg,
    ed., Spiritual Well-Being: Sociological Perspec-
    tives (Washington, D.C.: University Press of Amer-
    ica, 1979).

4. See Robin M. Hendig, "Exposing the Myth of Senili-
    ty," New York Times Magazine, December 3, 1978.

5. Mc Kenzie, Ibid.

A MODEL CURRICULUM ON
POLICY, LAW, ADVOCACY AND AGING

By

James B. Boskey, Susan C. Hughes and Robert H. Manley

INTRODUCTION

The purpose of this course is to develop knowledge and skills with regard to public policy, law and advocacy in aging. The course is designed for either undergraduate or graduate programs, or a combination of both. A mixture of graduate and undergraduate students will even be acceptable. Appropriate adjustments may be made to the materials utilized, general approach and requirements depending on the level.

Needless to say, the subject matter of public policy and law with regard to aging is virtually limitless in scope. By the same taken, advocacy has innumerable facets. From the law/policy perspective, the approach of the course, as indicated in the model syllabus, is to deal with those areas thought to be the most salient in the medium-term future. As to advocacy, the focus is on the development of skills, both to straighten out particular problems as they are encountered and to undertake policy changes when necessary or appropriate. It is intended that the students learn not only how to utilize the advocacy techniques themselves, but to transmit these skills to the elderly and to others involved with servicing the elderly. In situations in which specialized advocacy techniques are required, for instance in achieving either ad hoc outcomes or more general policy change through the courts, the emphasis is on developing understanding as to the best type of advocacy to be used and how qualified advocates can be identified, retained and assisted.

The stress of fostering student awareness of the importance of assisting the aging themselves in developing advocacy capabilities is regarded as an important aspect of the course approach since, to every extent possible, the intention is to communicate values in which the aging are seen, not as persons for whom services must be performed, but as persons to be assisted in achieving the fullest respect in the community and in achieving the fullest status in performing for themselves the ongoing tasks of life. At the same time, the course seeks to sensitize students to special ethnic, gender and social class problems and challenges likely to be encountered in pursuing advocacy in the aging context.

As indicated in the model syllabus, the course structure is one in which a focus on advocacy in various contexts - legislative, judicial, administrative, etc. - is juxtaposed against the particular substantive aspects of aging policy/law, as for instance, in regard to income maintenance, housing and health.

Utilization of case studies and simulations in the classroom is proposed in order to further student understanding of the realities with regard to advocacy in aging, to enhance a sense of personal involvement, and to sharpen policy/law analysis skills and advocacy skills. The research projects and in-class reports of the same are based upon the same rationale. It is recommended that consideration be given to inviting members of the aging community and those working in the field of aging to attend class sessions devoted to case study analysis, simulations and presentations of research reports and to participate through commentary.

While the model syllabus is premised on a fifteen week semester structure, with two seventy-five minute classes per week, it can easily be adapted to other teaching formats. The type and number of examinations and the determination of the weight to be accorded to each will necessarily depend on the level of instruction at which the course is offered, as will the weight of the other elements of instruction.

SYLLABUS OUTLINE

This course is designed to assist the student in understanding policy and legal contexts of aging in developing his or her abilities for advocacy and assisting others in developing advocacy skills in this area.

Advocacy is seen as involving two dimensions, one in which attempts are made to resolve conflicts on an ad hoc (per case) basis, and the other in which the goal is more general policy change in a preferred direction.

The two primary groups targeted for assistance in the development of advocacy techniques are the elderly themselves and those employed in the public or private sector and whose work involves regularly dealing with matters affecting the elderly.

There follows a week by week overview of the major elements of the course:

Week of
Semester

1. <u>Introduction:</u> The purpose of the course. Concepts of pressure or special interest groups in the political process. Nature of the aging process among the elderly population in the United States. Role of the advocate in the aging context. Institutions relevant to aging policy and law. Interaction between federal and state levels and limitations on powers at each level. Experience in using statute material with the Older Americans Act as the focal point.

2. <u>An Overview of Policy and Law in Aging:</u> Nature of the public policy process. Relationship between policy and law. Historical development of policy/law as to aging in the United States. Comparative and international dimensions of aging policy. Categorical as opposed to general delivery services systems approaches. Ethnic and

gender problems and aspects with respect to aging
policy/law. Policy objectives of the Older Americans Act of 1965 (as amended). Federal/state/
local interrelationships fostered by the Older
Americans Act.

3. The Nature of Advocacy: Analysis of factual
    situations as an element of advocacy skills.
    Identifying problems and possible solutions.
    Determining applicable advocacy techniques.
    Special advocacy problems involving ethnic min-
    orities and women, individually or as a group.
    Provisions of the Older Americans Act especial-
    ly relevant to the advocacy function.

4. Income Maintenance Problems: The range of devices
    established under federal and state law for the
    purposes of income maintenance, with special refer-
    ence to the elderly. Psychological impact of the
    end of employment status. Relevance of the Age
    Discrimination in Employment Act (ADEA) of 1967.
    Historical and comparative perspective of income
    for the elderly. Analysis of the Social Security
    Act of 1935 (as amended) and of the Employment
    Retirement Income Security Act (ERISA) of 1974.
    Welfare-type federal and state programs. Food
    stamps and other indirect supplements.

5. Legislative Advocacy: Nature of legislative ad-
    vocacy. Role of legislation in establishing so-
    cial service systems and in accomplishing change.
    Scope and limitations of legislative power. Leg-
    islative process. Role of the courts in interpre-
    tation. Interest group involvement. Techniques
    for statutory analysis and drafting. Exercise in
    bill drafting.

6. Housing: Interests of the elderly as affected in
    residential experiences ranging from "autonomy"
    to "institutional care" situations. Food and
    other support programs to facilitate the mainten-
    ance of autonomous living conditions. Tax aspects
    of housing. Legal barriers, including zoning, to
    group living arrangements. Nursing home manage-
    ment and regulation. Advocacy approaches to housing
    including long-term care ombudsman programs.

7. Administrative Advocacy: The nature of administrative agencies and their relationships to the legislative bodies and the courts. Delegation of legislative powers to administrative agencies including legitimacy of such delegations. Various functions of such agencies, including problems associated with conflict among functions. Scope and impact of administrative procedures acts at federal and state levels. Advocacy in administrative agencies, whether individually or in a group. Detailed examination of the administrative system for a particular state. "Moot" or simulation of an administrative quasi-judicial proceeding.

8. Health Care Problems: Special needs of the elderly with respect to medical care. Economic problems of access to services. Preventive health aspects. Medicare and Medicaid systems, including problems of the elderly with utilization of such programs. Health Maintenance Organizations (HMO) and other alternative approaches to the delivery of health care. Problem analysis as to administrative advocacy with respect to the Medicare system.

9. Advocacy in the Private Sector: Dealing with non profit and profit-oriented entities, whether of the type whose elientele is primarily the elderly or the type whose business takes it into contact with the elderly as part of the general population. Means of approaching and influencing operations and policies of private sector entities. Application of advocacy techniques in particular case situations.

10. Physical Safety and Recreation: Reasons for special risks of harm for the elderly. Problems associated with juvenile criminal activity. Abuse in the institutional setting. Abuse of the elderly by family members. Use of advocacy techniques in preventing or minimizing abuse, including legislative, judicial and administrative options. Recourse to civil and criminal protection options.

Reduced or free fee recreational and cultural programs. Development of community organization resources to provide protection. Related problems with reference to transportation. Volunteer service opportunities, including opportunities to act as advocates to the older person.

11. Judicial Advocacy: Courts as a menas of obtaining relief from wrongs and as a mans of affecting policy. Structure of the court system as to both civil and criminal actions. Alternatives to court action, including mediation and arbitration. Role of attorneys in and out of court. Functions of community legal service and legal referral programs. Concept of test case litigation. Class action suits. Focus on particular situations in which judicial advocacy might be particularly appropriate.

12.
& Case Studies and Simulations: In-class utiliza-
13. tions of case studies and simulations as approach to development of advocacy competence with reference to the contexts and aspects considered in the preceding weeks of the course.

14. Reports on Research: Oral presentations by students based on their written research reports prepared in connection with the course requirements. Research reports should demonstrate a capability for relating one or more aging policy contexts to advocacy techniques.

15. Concluding Aspects: Completion of presentations by students on research areas. Integrative final discussions pertaining to the goals of the course. Course evaluations.

WEEK BY WEEK DETAILED SYLLABUS

WEEK 1

INTRODUCTION

In the first class, students are introduced to the
purpose of the course, namely to develop knowledge and
skills for accomplishing change in public and private
institutions on behalf of an identified clientele in
the aging policy/law context. The concept of pressure
or special interest groups in the political process is
considered. An overview of the nature of the aging
population in the United States, with special emphasis
on the problems of poverty among the aging population,
the need for a sense of community in both the urban and
non-urban environment, and the relationship between the
aging component of the population and other segements
of the population is presented.

Emphasis is placed on the role of the advocate and
the relationship between the advocate and the client
in the aging context. The advocate representing the
real and perceived interests of the client is em-
phasized and the problem of distinguishing these categories is noted for additional consideration later in
the course. The range of advocacy roles is indicated
again with emphasis on the fact that these matters will
be further detailed in the remainder of the course.

Finally, included in the introduction is discussion of course assignments and expectations regarding
student work.

The second class begins the examination of the
structure of institutions in the United States society
impining on the elderly. This will include a survey
of the "legal" institutions, especially courts and
legislatures, with a brief introduction to their struc-
tures and functions. The relationship of the executive
branch of the government (including the bureaucracy) to
the legislative and judicial branches is also considered. The analysis continues with an introduction to
the scope and interest action of federal and state

powers, including discussion of limitations on federal
authority and ways of avoiding these limitations
through the use of voluntary funding procedures.

This is followed by a more detailed examination
of the roles of the courts and legislatures, with some
special emphasis on debunking the view that the United
States Suprement Court provides a forum for correction
of all injustices rather than having what are essentially more narrowly defined functions. Limitations on
legislative powers are discussed and the relationship
between state and federal legislation is considered in
the area of aging. Sections of the Older Americans
Act of 1965 (as amended) are examined in order to
provide some idea of how to read a statute. The role
of the court in statutory interpretation is brought
out in examples pertaining to the Act.

References: "The Aging of America: Questions for
a Four-Generation Society." Joseph Califano, Jr., in
Planning for the Elderly issue of the Annals of the
American Academy of Political and Social Science (July
1978; Chapter 1, "Social Work and the Law: An Over-
view" Chapter 2, Use of Legal References and Materials"
Chapter 16, "Legal Problems of the Aged," in Social
Work and the Law, by Donald Brieland and John Lemmon
(St. Paul: West Publishing Co., 1977); Older Americans
Act of 1965 (as amended), Title 42, USCA, Sections 3001,
et seq,; Older Americans Act: A Staff Summary, Select
Committee on Aging, U. S. House of Representatives,
Comm. Pub. No. 96-185, Revised July 1979; United States
Constitution, especially Articles I and III and the
Tenth Amendment.

WEEK 2
AN OVERVIEW OF POLICY AND LAW AS TO AGING

This section begins with a discussion of the nature of the public policy process, with public policy defined in terms of an authoritative determination of goals for society and of the means for achieving these goals. Consideration of the three primary phases of the policy process - formulation, implementation and evaluation - as well as the relationship between law and policy, is undertaken, note being made that policy is often, but not always, expressed in the form of law.

The historical development of policy/law as to aging is then discussed, with special emphasis to the shift of state level to federal level initiatives in the 1930's. Potential shifting in a reverse direction is also considered. The adoption of the Social Security Act in 1935 is viewed as a major transition point. The mid-1960's, with adoption in 1964 of the Economic Opportunity Act, launching the War on Poverty, and, in 1965, the adoption of the Older Americans Act, is likewise discussed, along with such programs as Medicare and Medicaid. The increasing concern with the viability of such programs as Social Security is also discussed as well as the impact of such political policies as the attempts to return much of the federal power to the states.

The second class begins with attention focused on the comparative and international dimensions of aging policy. Trends at the global level, especially as to policy developing within the United Nations and its specialized agencies, and within nation-states other than the United States, will be considered.

Discussion will then turn to distinctions between the two basic policy/law approaches affecting the condition of the elderly; i.e., those focusing specifically on the aging population (e.g., Older Americans Act) and those which impact on society in general, or towards a segment of the population that includes many of the elderly (e.g., the Economic Opportunity Act).

Attention then turns to ethnic and gender problems and aspects with regard to policy/law, with particular attention paid to the situations faced by the black. Hispanic and American Indian elderly, as well as discrimination faced by elderly women. Consideration is also given to the question of the extent to which the elderly as a group are victimized by negative stereotyping and the policy implications of such attitudes.

The second class concludes with an analysis of the policy objectives of the Older/Americans Act as well as of the complex of federal/state/local relationships fostered by the Act in pursuing these objectives.

References: An Introduction to the Study of Public Policy, Charles O. Jones (Belmont, CA.: Duxbury Press, 1977); Growing Old in America, David Fischer (New York: Oxford University Press, 1977), especially Chapter 4, "Old Age Becomes a Social Problem"; "AoA-Federal Focal Point for Action of Older Americans," Aging, May 1975; The Whole Person After 60; Issues in Intergovernmental Planning (Lexington, KY: Council of State Governments, 1977); The Older American: Issues in States Service (Lexington, KY: Council of State Governments, 1976); Social Services in the United States-Policies and Programs, Sheila Kammerman and Alfred Kahn (Philadelphia, PA: Temple University Press, 1976), especially Chapter devoted to "Community Services for the Aged," Chapter 9, Part I, "Minorities," in Developments in Aging:1978, Part I, Report of the Special Committee on Aging, U.S. Senate, published in 1979 as Report No. 96-55; "A Generation of Black People" and "Help for the Minority Aged" in The New Old: Struggling for Decent Aging, Ronald Gross, Beatrice Gross and Sylvia Seidman, eds. (Garden City, NY: Anchor Books, 1978); Older Women: A Workshop Guide (Washington, D.C.: National Commission on the Observance of International Women's Year, 1977); Chapter 4, "Treatment of Men and Women," in Social Security: Promise and Reality, Rita Ricardo Campbell (Stanford, CA: Hoover Institution Press, Stanford University, 1977); Emerging Aging Network - A Directory of State and Area Agencies on Aging,

Select Committee on Aging, U.S. House of Representatives, Washington, D.C., 1978; Reauthorization of the Older Americans Act: 1981, Hearing before the Subcommittee on Human Services of the Select Committee on Aging, U.S. House of Representatives, October 15, 1980, Ninety-Sixth Congress, Publication No. 96-248; International Directory of Organizations Concerned With the Aging, United Nations Department of Economic and Social Affairs, ST/ESA/63, New York, 1977; The Aging: Trends and Policies, United Nations Department of Economic and Social Affairs, ST/ESA/22, New York, 1975.

THE NATURE OF ADVOCACY

This week is dedicated to providing the student with an overview of the levels at which advocacy can function and the different styles of advocacy that are possible and accepted.

The study is commenced by presenting a model case of an elderly couple who face many problems and suggesting that the students should consider how many problems could be resolved. An example of the type of case study is as follows:

> Ann and Ben Charles live in a medium sized United States city. He is 78 years of age and she is 73. Until his retirement at age 65, Ben worked for a major brewery; Ann was employed in the ladies garment industry until her retirement at age 65. They have two children, married and living in separate parts of the United States, both over 1500 miles from their parents. The Charles' own a small house (clean but in a state of disrepair) in an area that has become increasingly dangerous in terms of street theft and breaking and entering homes. They receive Social Security benefits and each of them receives a pension. The amount of money that they receive barely enables them to survive. They have recently received word that their taxes on the property are to be increased by 15%. (Inflation has already cut their food budget to the bone.) In addition, both of them need substantial medical treatment. They are both taking prescription drugs, as a result of which they have become increasingly unable to cope with daily chores.

The first question asked of the students is to identify the problems that these people face. As the problems are identified, the students are encouraged to notice the overlap in causes between the different problems and to see how the problems build up by a process of reinforcement. Once the majority of problems have been identified, discussion is directed to the manner in which various problems can be solved.

The first problem to be dealt with is that of housing. The students are asked to look at the alternatives that may be available for the couple. Specific problems examined include:

1. Repair to the house.
2. Cost of taxes on the house.
3. Problem of increasing area crime.
4. Progressive frailty of the couple and and difficulty in caring for themselves.

The students are then encouraged to look for different ways in which problems could be resolved. The student should consider such alternatives as:

1. Nursing homes
2. Moving in with married children
3. Developing linkages with other elderly persons in the community
4. Homemaker services
5. Tax relief
6. Establishment of neighborhood improvement associations
7. Increased police attention to the area
8. Support for repair to the house

Each of them should be discussed to demonstrate the advantages and disadvantages as an alternative.

The same process is then followed with regard to other problems that the couple faces. Once it is evident that the students have the concept of problem analysis in hand at a basic level, attention should turn, usually in the second class, to possible roles for the advocate in this situation.

In looking at possible roles for the advocate, the students should be encouraged to examine all possibilities, problems and solutions. Appropriate questions to ask include:

1. Who might be approached to help solve a particular problem?
2. Are there groups of individuals who could be brought together to win support for solutions?

3. Are solutions available through the legislature, the courts, private or public agencies or other means?

In the course of this discussion, the student is provided with the idea of the range of advocacy techniques. Discussion should focus, at a minimum, on legislative and agency advocacy, coalition building, self-help groups, etc. In addition, attention may be focused on the court as problem solver, with suitable changes in the facts presented, and on individual charity and private charitable organizations.

After concluding discussion of the particular case attention should be given to special advocacy problems likely to be encountered with respect to minorities and women and as to the older person, either individually or in a group sense. The session will end with consideration of aspects of the Older Americans Act (as amended) that are relevant to advocacy and of advocacy programs developed under the Act's impetus.

References: The Law and Aging Manual (Washington, D.C.: Legal Research and Services for the Elderly, National Council of Senior Citizens, 1976), especially Chapter 2, "Law and Aging: What are the Issues?" and Chapter 3, "Law and Aging: How can Resources Best be Used"; "Legal Services for the Poor," Chapter 24 in Brieland and Lemmon, Social Work and the Law; A Short Review of the Paralegal Movement and the Growth of Other Non-Lawyer Representation (Washington, D.C.: National Paralegal Institute, National Public Law Training Center, 1977).

WEEK 4
INCOME MAINTENANCE PROBLEMS

The purpose of this week's coverage is to introduce the student to a wide range of income maintenance
devices existing under federal and state law, especially as they relate to the elderly. The discussion should
include the Social Security system, private pension
programs, regulation of the above by federal and state
legislatures, welfare, food stamps, supplemental programs and special tax advantages available at a state
and federal level. In addition, the Federal Age Discrimination in Employment Act of 1967 is introduced,
including the 1978 amendments extending mandatory retirement restraints to age 70. This week consists of
mostly lectures to introduce the various programs.

The student is first brought to the realization
that the status of employment was a focal point and
that the loss of this signals the beginning of old
age. It can be pointed out that many of the problems
faced by the elderly can be related to the unavailabi-
lity of employment to them and analogy is made to similar problems faced by those barred from employment
by physical disability or other extraneous factors.
Factors specifically examined include the problems of
income maintenance, lack of self-esteem, need to keep
busy and be productive, etc.

Attention is then turned to specific forms of income maintenance that are available. A brief examination of the means of providing for the elderly in pre-
modern societies is undertaken, followed by an examination of the means of dealing with these problems in the
United States prior to the Social Security Act of 1935.

At this point, discussion focuses on the Social
Security Act and the scope of coverage of the Act as to
the aged. Emphasis is placed on both the rights of
workers and the rights of worker dependents, under the
Act. The effects of earnings limitations are discussed
and the variations in retirement age provisions analy-
zed. The students are given specific sections of the

101

Act with which to familiarize themselves to learn the
form in which federal statutes are written.

The next area of focus is that of private pensions.
A brief overview of the types of pension schemes is
provided, followed by an analysis of the Employment
Retirement Income Security Act (ERISA) and related
legislation and the effect on private schemes. In the
course of the discussion, students are introduced to
the administrative regulations promulgated under the
act. Some limited attention is given to the problems
of termination prior to vesting and the failing company in the context of pensions.

This is followed by a brief discussion on the
range of direct payment welfare schemes under federal
and state law. Basically, what is provided here is
an overview to suggest to the students the need for
further analysis in this area. In addition, food
stamps and other supplemental programs, such as Medicare, are touched on.

Finally, a brief discussion of the Age Discrimination in Employment Act (ADEA) of 1967 is undertaken,
with an analysis of the basic provisions and the kinds
of remedies that are available under the act.

References: The Rights of Older Persons - An Am-
erican Civil Liberties Union Handbook, Robert M. Brown
(New York, NY: Avon Books, 1979), especially Part 1,
"The Right to an Adequate Income"; Law of the Elderly,
Jerome A. Weiss, ed. (New York, NY: Practicing Law
Institute, 1977), especially Chapter 1, "Supplemental
Security Income (SSI) ",Chapter 5, "What Do You Get
With the Gold Watch?: An Analysis of the Employment
Retirement Income Security Act of 1974 ", Chapter 8,
"Age Discrimination in Employment ",and Chapter 12,
"Senior Citizens and the Tax Reform Act of 1976";
Rights of the Elderly and Retired, William A. Wishard
(San Francisco, CA: Cragmont Publications, 1978), es-
pecially Part I, "Income: Sources and Maintenance,"
Chapter 13, " Job Finding: Age Discrimination," and
Part V, " Other Rights and Benefits"; Social Work and
the Law, Brieland and Lemmon, Chapter 19; Mandatory
Retirement: The Social and Human Cost of Enforced Idle-
ness, Select Committee on Aging (Comm Pub No 95-91.).

WEEK 5
LEGISLATIVE ADVOCACY

The focus of this week's program is the nature of legislative advocacy and techniques of accomplishing change through legislative action. The student is introduced to the role of legislation in structuring social service systems and to the advantages and disadvantages of this route in accomplishing change. Also included is an introduction to the techniques of analysis and of drafting statutes.

Initially, consideration is given to the types of legislative bodies in the United States. While the primary focus is on federal and state legislatures, reference is made to the legislative powers of county and municipal governmental units. The scope of legislative power is discussed, with some emphasis on the limitations of legislation as a means of reform. Attention is also given to the importance of legislation of a fiscal nature and to the role of the courts in the interpretation of legislation. This is followed by a discussion of the process in which legislation is enacted. Emphasis is placed on the role of the lobbyist and the importance of understanding committee functions. It should be noted that in many cases, it may be good to bring in outside speakers (legislators, legislative staff members, interest group representatives, etc.) to participate in the discussion.

In the second class session, emphasis is placed on the analysis and drafting of legislation. While it is possible to use federal legislation, such as the Older Americans Act, for this purpose, it is generally more desirable to focus on an appropriate state statute such as the common state constitutional requirement of having legislation deal only with one subject. The selection of a piece of legislation can encourage the student's understanding of the subject matter. The legislation selected should include reference to other legislation, definitional clauses, etc., to provide the student with an understanding of the types of problems that can occur in statutory interpretation. It

103

may also be appropriate to introduce a judicial decision on statutory interpretation to demonstrate the techniques involved in this to the students.

In addition to the above, the student should be introduced to the use of compiled (annotated) statutes. A volume of annotated statutes should be selected and the student acquainted with the full range of secondary material that appears in such volumes, as well as the manner in whichthe legislation is categorized and distributed.

Finally, it may be appropriate to provide the students with an exercise in simple statute drafting. While the student is unlikely to develop an effective drafting technique from this exercise, it should provide the student with some understanding of the process. Student work on this exercise must be critiqued in detail to provide appropriate results.

Some subjects that might be considered for this exercise include:

    1. Nondiscrimination in housing
    2. Nondiscrimination in employment
    3. Driver's license retesting bill
    4. Bill providing for establishment
            of senior citizen centers

References: "The Legislative Process and Social Action," in Brieland and Lemmon, Social Work and the Law; Legislative and Administrative Processes (Cases and Materials), Hans Linde and George Bunn (Mineola, NY: Foundation Press, 1974); Legislative Law and Process in a Nutshell, Jack Davies (St. Paul, MN: West Publishing Company, 1975), especially Chapter 3, "Advocacy in the Legislature," Chapter 5, "Bill drafting," Chapter 6, "Legislative Policy Making," Chapter 13, "Statutory Interpretation," and Chapter 14, "For the People"; Congressional Procedures and Policy Process, Walter J. Oleszek (Washington, DC: Congressional Quarterly Press, 1978); Interest Groups, Lobbying and Policymaking, Norman J. Ornsteing and Shirley Elder (Washington, DC: Congressional Quarterly Press, 1978); Legislative Problems of the Elderly (Washington: National Council of Senior Citizens, 1971).

Attention is focused on interests of the elderly
as affected by different types of residential situations, ranging from virtually complete autonomy in a
mized age population setting to intensive institutional care limited to older persons.

At an early point, consideration is given to the
advantages and disadvantages of homogeneous communities
for the elderly. The students' attention is then directed to such residential situations as nursing homes.
After the group has (usually) come to the conclusion
that this approach is not desirable except in cases in
which no viable alternative is available, attention is
drawn to the retirement community as an option.

Discussion is focused on the question of why a substantial proportion of older Americans live in homogeneous rather than in the heterogeneous communities in
which they have previously been living, especially when
cost is not the controlling factor.

Following this discussion, attention is focused on
particular problems faced by the aging adult in achieving the type of residential situation desired. Attention is paid to special property tax breaks for the
elderly - their advantages and disadvantages - and other
programs created to ease the financial situation of the
elderly with respect to housing such as transportation
programs, assistance in meeting utility costs, etc.

Attention is then turned to autonomous living
problems and the frail or near-frail elderly. Support
programs for autonomous living are discussed, including
companionship and contact programs, homemaker programs,
shopping assistance and food preparation and delivery
programs. The relationship between housing and transportation programs is also considered.

In the second session, attention is turned to collective living arrangements. Discussion focuses on
senior citizen housing under federal funding, with some
discussion of barriers to unofficial collective living,
including some zoning restrictions. Attention is given

to the physical needs of the elderly, including barrier free construction and access to services.

Finally, the concept of the nursing home is considered. A brief history of profit and non-profit nursing home approaches is provided and the problems facing both those residing in them and those operating them are examined. Reasons for the defects in operation are considered and the means of correcting them are explored.

Throughout, the classes held for this week, advocacy approaches, both for the individual and the groups of elderly, in relation to achieving satisfactory housing and related conditions,are dealt with. Special attention is given to the long-term care ombudsman program provided for in the Older American Act (as amended).

References: Chapter 2, Part C, "Housing", in the Law and Aging Manual; Chapter 12, "Housing Problems and Solutions", in Wishard, Rights of the Elderly and Retired; The Pursuit of Dignity: New Living Alternatives for the Elderly, Bert Kruger Smith(Boston, MA: Beacon Press, 1977); Nursing Homes: A Citizens' Action Guide, Linda Horn and Elma Griesel (Boston, MA: Beacon Press, 1977); "Nursing Homes: A First Step to Change", Chapter 3 in For the People: A Consumer Action Handbook, Joanne Manning Anderson (Reading, MA: Addison-Wesley, 1977); Chapter 7, "Nursing Homes", in Brown, The Rights of Older Persons - An ACLU Handbook; Chapter 9, "Nursing Home Law", by Philip Gassel in Weiss, Law of the Elderly; "Long Term Policy Issues: Alternatives to Institutional Care," Faye G. Abdellah, in Planning for the Elderly issues, Annals, July 1978. "Regulation of Nursing Homes: A Case Study," by Charles J. Hynes, in Regulating Health Care: The Struggle for Control, Arthur Levin, ed. Proceedings of The Academy of Political Science, Vol. 33, No. 4 (New York, NY: The Academy of Political Science, 1980).

ADMINISTRATIVE ADVOCACY

This week's program is intended to introduce the student to the structure of the administrative system, and to the ways of influencing its operation, with special reference to problems affecting the aging.

The first session begins with a description of the nature of administrative agencies and their relationship with legislative bodies and the courts. The concept of delegation of power by the legislature is discussed, as is the issue of limitation of power.

Attention is then turned to the three different functions of administrative agencies: rule-making, adjudicative and operational. Particular attention is paid to the difference in these functions in carrying out goals. The students are introduced to the administrative procedure acts (federal, state or both) and discussion focuses on the effects of these acts on all three agency functions.

The question of advocacy with reference to the administrative agency is then discussed. Techniques of influencing agency action are considered in relation to each of the three functions of the agency and the likelihood of influencing agency action by various approaches considered. The distinction between advocacy for the individual client and collective advocacy is considered in this context, as is the possibility of role conflict in the advocacy process.

There follows in the second session a detailed examination of the administrative system in a particular state. The range of agencies is discussed with special reference to those having substantial impact on the aging. The manner in which agencies interact in the provision of services and in performing regulatory functions is considered. This is followed by a brief "moot" or simulation of an administrative quasi-judicial hearing to provide the student with an idea of the type of procedure that is followed and the kinds of results that can be achieved.

References: Kenneth Culp Davis, Administrative
Law: Cases, Text, Problems (St. Paul, MN.: West Pub-
lishing Co. 1977); Kenneth Culp Davis, Administrative
Law and Government, second edition (St. Paul, MN. West
Publishing Co., 1975) Kenneth Culp Davis, Administra-
tive Law Text (St. Paul, MN. West Publishing Company.
1972) Ernest Gellhorn and Barry B. Boyer, Administra-
tive Law and Process in a Nutshell (St. Paul, MN: West
Publishing Co., 1981); Walter Gellhorn and Clark Byse,
Administrative Law: Cases and Comments (Mineola, N.Y.:
Foundation Press, 1974); Hans Linde and George Bunn.
Legislative and Administrative Processes (Mineola, N.Y.:
Foundation Press, 1974); Glen Robinson, Ernest Gellhorn
and Harold Bruff, The Administrative Process (St. Paul
MN.: West Publishing Co., 1980); Donald D. Barry and
Harold R. Whitcombe, The Legal Foundations of Public
Administration (St. Paul, MN.: West Publishing Company,
1981).

WEEK 8
HEALTH CARE PROBLEMS

This week provides an overview of the relationship
of the aging population and the health care system.
Attention is focused on the economic problems of access
to health care and the provision of preventative services.

The session begins with a brief survey of the
special needs of the aging population with regard to
medical care. Discussion focuses on acute and chronic
care as well as treatment outside these categories.
Attention is given also to the preventative aspects of
medical care for the elderly and to nutrition as a key
dimension of a "positive" health approach. Brief discussion is had of the range of possible service providers and the economic and psychological consequences of
a particular selection.

Attention is then focused on the nature of the
Medicare and Medicaid systems as they are available
to the elderly. Intensive examination of the quali-
fication for medical services under these programs is
undertaken, followed by an analysis of the types of
service provided. Problems as to obtaining adequate
service are considered and the response of the medical
and related professions to the Medicare and Medicaid
programs evaluated.

The discussion then turns to other forms of medi-
cal-related programs for the elderly, including prescription assistance and health screening. Concepts
such as of the H.M.O. (Health Maintenance Organization)
and other alternative forms of care are also considered.
Transportation needs of the elderly in obtaining health
care, especially where services are fragmented, are
dealt with.

A problem involving administrative advocacy under
the Medicare system is presented. As discussion develops, consideration is given to selected statutory and
rule provisions related to the problem.

References:Chapter 2, part B, "Health and Medical
Services" in The Law and Aging Manual; Part 2, "Health
and Medical Services" in Wishard, Rights of the Elderly
and Retired; chapter 6, "An Advocate's Guide to the
Medicare Program", Patricia A. Butler, in Weiss, Law of
the Elderly; chapter 7, "Medicare" and chapter 8,
"Medicaid" in Brown, The Rights of Older Persons--An
ACLU Handbook; chapter 5, "The Elderly and Disease--
Medicare and Medicaid--Help and Hinderance" in Lawrence
Corey, Michael Epstein and Steven E. Saltman, Medicine
in a Changing Society, (St. Louis, C. V. Mosby Co.,
1977). "Who is Entitled to Medicare?", Arthur Abraham
and David Kopelman, in The Practical Lawyer, Vol. 25,
No. 8, December 1979; "An Evaluation of Regulatory
Standards and Enforcement Devices in the Nursing Home
Industry," James L. Miller, Akron Law Review, Vol. 13:4,
Spring 1980; Nursing Home Care in the United States:
Failure in Public Policy, Subcommittee on Long-term
Care of the Senate Special Committee on Aging, S.Rep.
No. 93-1420, 93rd Congress, Second Session (1974);
The Politics of Medicine, Theodore R. Marmor (Chicago,
IL: Aldine Publishing Company, 1973; The Nation's
Health, Philip R. Lee, Nancy Brown and Ida Red, eds.
(San Francisco, CA: Boyd & Fraser Publishing Co., 1981),
especially Chapter 12, "A Social Science Perspective:
Research on Aging," and "Health Policy, Social Policy,
and the Health of the Aging: A Prelude to a Decade of
Disaster," by H. Jack Geiger; Human Rights and Health
Care Law, Eugene I. Pavalon (New York, NY: American
Journal of Nursing Publishing Co, 1980), Part 5, "Death
with Dignity,"(see especially Introduction and Chapter
15, "Duty to Prolong Life Reexamined.")

WEEK 9
ADVOCACY IN THE PRIVATE SECTOR

During this week the study of two different ditua-
tions will be undertaken:
1) advocacy with regard to non-profit or profit-
   making entities particularly concerned with
   the problems of aging and
2) advocacy with regard to organizations that deal
   with public in general, and thus for which
   dealings with senior citizens are not a distinct class of transactions (i.e. banks, super-
   markets, utility companies, insurance carriers,
   etc.).

The first session deals with the aging-oriented
entity. The impact of the profit making or non-
profit nature of the agency is discussed as is the
range of functions undertaken by such agencies. Sources
of funding for the rendering of services are also considered.

From an advocacy standpoint the means of approaching such agencies and influencing their policies and
operations becomes the point of focus. The manner of
making contact, types of reforms that may be sought,
etc. are examined. A comparison is drawn between advocacy with reference to such private agencies and
advocacy with regard to their public counterparts.

The second session is directed towards advocacy
with the normal commercial entity. Particular entities are selected as the basis for the discussion and
particular problems are identified. Some problems
which may be used are:

1. The inability of an aging person to get to
   a bank to make and pursue a loan application.
2. Difficulties for an aging person in transport-
   ing home groceries from a retail store.

The students examine the nature of the problems and
possible ways of resolving them. They are reminded of
the dictum that the best way to solve a problem may be
not to "raise the bridge", but to "lower the river",

(look for alternative, less costly means of accomplishing a particular purpose). Means of influencing such organizations are considered and approaches to resolving the problems are discussed. This is then put into a general context for the resolution of a wide range of similar problems, including such issues as obtaining insurance for the elderly etc.

References: Part 4, "Consumer Protection" in Wishard Rights of the Elderly and Retired; chapter 20; "Consumer Protection" in Brieland and Lemmon, Social Work and the Law; chapter 13, "The Elderly Consumer and Fraud Schemes", Stephen A. Newman and Karin L. Straus, in Weiss, in Weiss, Law of the Elderly; chapter 1, "How to Stop the Rx Ripoff", chapter 5, "Fighting for Lower Utility Bills", and part 3, "Grocery Projects" in Anderson, For the People-A Consumer Action Handbook.

WEEK 10
PHYSICAL SAFETY AND RECREATION

This week introduces the matter of physical security for the older person in the context of both the residential and the community setting as well as that of recreational (including cultural and avocational)needs.

The first session begins with a discussion of the reasons that the aging are often at risk of physical harm. In the community setting, the inability of the aging to defend themselves in many cases is discussed and the problem of the availability and visibility of the aging as victims of juvenile criminal activity focused upon. Problems of institutional abuse are considered, with an analysis of the reasons that such abuse occurs, the types of abuse that are seen and the indications that such abuse is occurring. This is followed by an examination of the problem of abuse of the elderly by family members. Both physical and psychological absue are considered, and the reasons for such abuse occurring analysed. To the extent feasible a profile of the abusing family is developed.

The focus then turns to means of preventing physical and psychological abuse. The range of advocacy techniques which can be brought to bear are disaussed as are legislative, administrative, and judicial options. Attention is given to the scope of criminal and civil law protections available for the aging person and the advantages and disadvantages of the legal route are considered.

Community organization techniques that may be used to bring together outside forces to provide further protection are dealt with. This is supported by discussion of the relevance of daily or weekly contact programs that allow the aging person a regular channel for the registration of viewpoints as to a sense of insecurity, or specific complaints.

With regard to recreation,programs for reduced or free entrance fees for cultural and athletic events and educational development activities, as well as related transportation problems, are considered.

Attention is also given to volunteer service opportunities, both paying and non-paying, including opportunities for service as advocates for older persons, both in structured situations, such as is provided by work with an association of senior citizens and in more informal or self-generated contexts.

References: In Search of Security: A National Prospective on Elderly Victimization, report by Subcommittee on Housing and Consumer Interests of the Select Committee on Aging, U. S. House of Representatives, April 1977 (Comm. Pub. No. 95-87); Research into Crimes Against the Elderly (Part 1, Joint Hearings before the Select Committee on Aging (and other committees), U. S. House of Representatives, January 31, 1978,) (Comm.Dec. No. 95-122); Violent Crime Against the Elderly, a briefing by the Select Committee on Aging, U. S. House of Representatives, June 1978 (Comm. Pub. No. 95-146); Leisure Activities for the Aged", M. Powell Lawton, in Planning for the Elderly issue, Annals, July 1978; Avocation and Employment Needs of Retired Persons,hearing before the Select Committee on Aging, U. S. House of Representatives February 11, 1978, Hackettstown, N. J. (Comm. Pub. No. 95-162);The Santa Cruz Story-- Senior Citizens Legal Service (Older People Serving Older People in a Legal Setting), Wanda R. Collins, Terrence M. Donnelly, Claire McAdams (San Francisco: California Rural Legal Assistance Office and National Senior Citizens Law Center, 1973).

WEEK 11
JUDICIAL ADVOCACY

This week introduces the student to the courts as a means of obtaining relief from various types of wrongs and of influencing policy. The focus is on limitations on judicial power and effectiveness and the fact that the courts are, in most cases, a "last resort" for the redress of grievances.

The structure of the court system is discussed and the role of civil and criminal litigation distinguished. Emphasis is placed on the small claims court for the resolution of civil disputes, and access to that court is considered. Alternatives to court action such as mediation and arbitration under the Community Disputes Service of the American Arbitration Association are dealt with.

This is followed by a discussion of the role of the attorney in and out of the court system. The appropriate use and selection of counsel is considered, and the importance of counsel to an effective advocacy effort evaluated. The role of community legal service and of legal referral programs is indicated and the limitations of these approaches brought out.

Some discussion is focused on the concept of test case litigation, including the problems and advantages of this type of action. The concept of the class action is considered as is the use of legal counsel before certain administrative agencies for the achievement of majore rule development and change.

Attention is then directed to specific topic areas within the law that are of particular importance to the aging population and to the use of judicial advocacy in these contexts include:
1. Age discrimination in employment
2. Consumer protection
3. Rent increases and tenant evictions
4. Increases in assessments and in tax rates on homes
5. Undue influence in obtaining gifts and bequests

References: "When Courts Should Make Policy: an In-
stitutional Approach" in Public Law and Public Policy;
John A. Gardiner, editor, (New York: Praeger Publishers,
1977); chapter 4, "The American Judiciary" in John A.
Straayer and Robert D. Wrinkle, Introduction to Ameri-
can Government and Policy, (Columbus, Ohio: Charles
Merrill Publishing Co., 1975); Public Interest Law--
An Economic and Institutional Analysis, Burton A.
Weisbred, (Berkeley: University of California Press,
1978), especially chapters 3,8,9, 12 and 14; chapter 9,
"Guardianship and Civil Commitment" in Brown, The
Rights of Older Persons--An ACLU Handbook: chapter 10,
"Protective Services for the Elderly: The Limits of
Parens Patriae", Peter M. Horstman in Weiss, The Law
of the Elderly.

WEEKS 12 & 13
CASE STUDIES AND SIMULATIONS

In these two weeks, it is proposed that case studies and simulations be utilized as approaches to the
development of advocacy competence in reference to the
contexts and aspects previously considered.

The following case studies are among the many fact
situations which could be employed for the purposes of
such in-class exercises:

1.   A public utility company providing electric and
gas service in a given area has just petitioned for a
14% across-the-board increase in rates to consumers.
A non-profit organization comprised of senior citizens
residing in the area wishes to prevent or minimize the
increase.   In the simulation, the class is divided up,
with one or more students taking roles as members of
the board of directors of the senior citizen organization, as officials of the utility company, as members
of the Public Utility Commission at the state level,
as attorneys with the Department of the Public Advocate at the state level, as individual aggrieved seniors who wish to serve as self-advocates, and as members of the court passing upon the validity of the
Public Utility Commission's administrative decision
in the matter.   The course instructor (s) will serve
as "updaters" of the factual situation as events pro-
ceed.   The simulation is played out, up to and including the court's determination as to the validity.

2.   The class is asked to "brainstorm" the problem
of reducing crime and other threats to the physical
security of elderly residents in a given area.   Among
the problems faced are: groups of teenagers who have
been victimizing older persons, sometimes to obtain
money, sometimes for no apparent reason; individual
dogs and groups of dogs on the loose which, by barking
and snapping, throw fear into seniors out for walks;
sidewalks in front of private residences which are so
broken up that they constitute a hazard to all pedes-
trians, but especially to those who are a bit frail;
and street crossings where "near misses" from passing
vehicles are a normal occurrence due to inoperative

117

traffic signals. Emphasis in the brain-storming sessions is to be placed upon various approaches to advocacy (including individual and group self-advocacy by senior citizens) in dealing with the problems encountered.

3. It has been learned that because in some instances federal funds received by state aging projects under Older Americans Act programs were inefficiently utilized, there is a substantial prospect that congress will reduce the level of appropriations by up to 1/3 for the coming year. Five different groups comprised of senior citizens have begun to organize state and national campaigns to show Senators and members of the House of Representatives what the effect of such cuts will be on services for the elderly as well as to inform public opinion in this regard. The class is to organize itself into five teams, one to advise each of the senior citizen groups in its campaign. Some teams will focus on state-level, others on national-level efforts. Each team reports its proposals back to the re-assembled class, at which point other team members are encouraged to provide critiques.

4. The class is informed that a group of about 150 older persons is living in a communal setting about 3/4 of an hour drive from the nearest town of any size. The housing and other aspects of the physical environment are quite satisfactory, but there is a great deal of boredom, which some members of the community attribute to lack of cultural and athletic activities to attend or participate in. It appears there is no recreational program and relatively little in the way of unorganized recreation, aside from watching television and talking. In addition, there is no organized religious group at or near the community. The class is asked to consider this situation and come up with specific approaches dealing with cultural, educational recreational and spiritual needs (including transportation aspects to the extent of their relevance) and to suggest strategies for seeing that the needs are met. The class should be encouraged to think about ways of involving the older persons themselves in the process of problem solving and of advocacy in pursuing the goals as they are defined.

5.   Each person in the class is given factual situations to react to. The assumption is that each is employed with a public or private agency primarily involved with serving the elderly. One student is told that
he/she is called by a "client" who is being evicted for
failure to pay the rent, another that his/her client
has not received the monthly social security check,
now 15 days overdue, another that Medicare refuses to
pay for certain hospital expenses of a client, and so
on. Students are encouraged to develop the ability
to identify "on the spot" either ways and means for
solving the problems or sources for information and
advice which could be sought by the agency employee,
the older person or both.

6.   A group of older persons living in a certain city
finds that there are no local organizations of seniors
with which they can affiliate. They desire such an
association, both for social purposes and to pool their
strength to achieve policy outcomes. The class is asked to help them develop an association. It is also
asked to advise on techniques for reaching other seniors in the area, on whether the association should obtain a charter from state or other officials, what its
structure should be, whether it faces any state or other
regulation of advocacy activities, and how to develop
effective advocacy, as well as social-recreational,
programs. Various task forces within the class tackle
particular aspects and report to the overall class,
which is regarded at that point as the senior group
that sought assistance. Members of the class, in roles
as persons in the senior group, question each task force, seeking additional details required and indicating
shortcomings perceived in the proposals.

7.   A senior citizens organization engaged in a campaign to obtain lower rates for gas and electricity
from the utilities finds that the media (newspapers,
radio, television, etc.) is almost universally unacco-
modating, if not downright hostile. Press releases are
seldom utilized, materials submitted responding to ed-
itorials in support of the utility position contra such
rate reductions are generally ignored and legislative
hearings at which the seniors testify for the reductions are scantily covered. All this is in sharp con-

trast to substantial media reference to anti-reduction
testimony. The class is asked to discuss and come up
with a series of approaches, whether involving legal,
public relations or other sanctioned techniques for
"turning around" the media "cold shoulder". In affecting public opinion and attitudes of administrators,
legislators, public utility commission members etc.,
other than through media impact.

8. The class is advised that a group of senior citizens has approached it wishing advice on "network"
building to further public policy advocacy on issues
affecting the elderly. Their particular policy concerns at the moment are in the areas of rent control
and stabilization of property tax rates as well as
utility costs, but they would like to be able to work
through networks on a range of policy issues. They
know very little about senior organizations other than
their own, which is strictly local in nature, and they
have not developed any techniques for working with
church and other organizations, or for identifying
other population groups (taxpayer associations, poverty organizations, ethnic-based organizations, etc.)
which might share their concerns. The class is asked to
come up with appropriate strategies for relating the
local senior citizen group to other groups with which
it has common cause, or who for whatever reason, will
be supportive of the group's interests.

9. Senior citizens in a given area report that there
has recently been a blitz of insurance salespersons
from several companies using high pressure tactics to
get them to take on "health insurance" coverage, in
addition to whatever coverage they now have. The sales
persons constantly point to the frailty of life, especially in the "golden years", asserting that without
protection seniors face doom, both in terms of health
and economic status. Given these facts, the class is
asked to arrive at the appropriate means for protecting the rights of the elderly confronted by this
campaign. Members divide into task force teams, which
report their proposed approaches to the overall group.

WEEK 14
REPORTS OF RESEARCH

It is anticipated that, for a course of this nature, many instructors will wish to utilize research projects, whether performed by individual students or "task force" student groups, as a means of developing knowledge and skills relative to the areas under consideration. Presumably, students would be advised that such reports should demonstrate capability for relating advocacy to one or more aging policy/law contexts. The following are examples of possible research reports:

1. A student or group of students could undertake a study of advocacy "competence" among older citizens. While the approach to design of such a study would vary from project to project, one possibility would be to explore two primary dimensions of "competence"; a) the extent to which the population group in question is informed on issues facing the elderly, on the state of existing policy/law, on trends in policy/law development and on the contexts (legislative, adminstrative, judicial) in which policies are formulated and implemented; b) the types of advocacy techniques that are available, either for individuals or groups, and their most appropriate use under various circumstances. The research could be conducted through a series of in-depth interviews with older persons, with information as to their background, educational, vocational and otherwise, obtained in order to facilitate analysis of factors which might correlate with higher or lower levels of competence in either or both dimensions.

2. A student or group of students could work on the construction of a model for aging policy/law in terms of the achievement, to the maximum extent feasible, of preferred goals. Such a project could either attempt to deal with all parameters of aging policy/law or be restricted to a given area, such as housing, health care or income maintenance. Presumably, the research report would indicate the extent to which the "ideal" policy had already been formulated and implemented, thus providing a benchmark for assessing "unfinished business".

121

3.   A student or group of students could prepare a
pamphlet for use by the elderly describing in some
detail the services available, from governmental and
non-governmental sources to them in a given municipa-
lity or other geographical area. They would be encouraged to utilize existing compendia of services
as prepared by area aging agencies, churches, social
service agencies, etc., but to improve on these in
terms of comprehensiveness and readability.

4.   A student or group of students could prepare a
"fact kit" for dissemination to media, legislators,
etc. in support of a campaign to obtain legislation
at state level providing a subsidy either for all
senior citizens or for those below a certain income
level, to assist in purchasing prescription drugs
when individual expenditures in a given calendar year
reach a certain level. (Other fact situations, involving other types of legislative campaigns, can be
used interchangeably).

5.   A student or group of students could undertake a
study of attitudes toward advocacy on behalf of the
elderly and as to the level of development of and competence for advocacy among persons in public and private agencies serving the aging. The extent to which
persons in such positions see advocacy, both in terms
of rectifying particular problems which are encountered and in accomplishing policy change, as part of their
primary responsibility, and their awareness of advocacy techniques appropriate to various circumstances,
could be explored through interviews. Analysis of
background information on the respondents obtained in
the interviews and as to the type of agency in which
they work, as well as the type of responsibility performed, might facilitate understanding of circumstances
conducive to development of positive attitudes regarding advocacy and of advocacy competence.

6.   A student or group of students could undertake
a study of comparative policy in dealing with problems
faced by the aging in several different nation-states
or among several states within the United States. The

122

research could be focused on either a broad spectrum of relevant issue areas or limited to only a few or even to one. Stated policies of the entities under consideration could be contrasted with "outcomes" in terms of such empirical indicators as housing units available per thousand, levels of income and life expectancy.

7.   A student or group of students could identify a policy area affecting the aging which they believed required legislative action. They could then draft pertinent legislation and prepare a letter to a member of the legislature requesting its introduction in bill form, as well as a statement in support of the bill to be utilized at hearings conducted by legislative committees considering the item.

8.   A student or group of students could undertake research regarding special problems faced by older persons who are members of ethnic minorities or by older omen (or older men). The research could be conducted primarily through library-based study through interviews with persons in the affected groups or through interviews with professionals working with such person (A combinational approach could also be employed.)

9.   A student or group of students could prepare a training manual to be utilized in developing advocacy skills either for persons whose work involves serving the elderly in a public or private agency context or for seniors themselves. The manual would seek to enhance understanding of advocacy in both an ad hoc (per individual case) sense and with regard to obtaining changes in overall policy. The students would be encouraged to prepare the manual in such a way that it would enhance advocacy competence in a variety of problem settings (housing, health, safety etc.) and in terms of dealing with administrative, legislative and perhaps, also judicial contexts.

WEEK 15
CONCLUDING ASPECTS

Initially, the week will be devoted to completion of reports of student research and critiques of these. Once this has been concluded, it will doubtless be useful to summarize, through lecture and discussion, findings and insights achieved during the course as to policy, law and advocacy in the field of aging and to identify those areas most in need of further development at national, state, local (and, for that matter, global), levels.

The final class activity could then be evaluation of the course, taking into account goals as stated in initial sessions and the extent to which in the succeeding sessions, including those devoted to case studies, simulation exercises and to research reports goal fulfillment was achieved.

BIBLIOGRAPHY

(A MODEL CURRICULUM ON POLICY, LAW, ADVOCACY AND AGING)

ADMINISTRATION

AoA Occasional Papers on Gerontology. No. 2: Human
Resources Issues in the Field of Aging (Homemaker/
Health Aide Services). Department of Health and
Human Services, DHEW Publ. No. 77-20086 (Washington,
D.C.: Government Printing Office, 1977).

"Casework with the Older Person and His Family," M.
Milloy, Social Casework 45: 450-456, October, 1964.

Consequences of Changing U.S. Population: Demographics
of Aging. Joint hearing of Select Committee on Population and Select Committee on Aging, U.S. House of
Representatives, Vol. I, May 24, 1978 (Washington,
D.C.: Government Printing Office, 1978).

Executive Ombudsman in the United States. Alan Wynev
(Berkeley, CA.: University of California Press, 1973).

Family, Bureaucracy and the Elderly. Ethel Shanas and
M. Sussman (Durham, NC.: Duke University Press, 1977)

Fragmentation of Services for the Elderly. Select Committee on the Aging, U. S. House of Representatives,
Committee Publication No. 95-93, April 4, 1977 (Washington, D.C.: Government Printing Office, 1977).

Handbook of American Aging Programs. Lorin Baumhover
and Jean Jones, ed. (Westport, CN: Greenwood Press,
1977).

Legal Problems of Hospital and Nursing Home Programs.
(New York, NY: Practicing Law Institute, 1974).

Old Age Institutions. Barbara Manard, et al. (Lexington, MA: Lexington Books, 1975).

Organization and Administration of Services Programs
to Older Americans. Richard Hardy and John Cull, eds.
(Springfield, IL: C.C. Thomas, 1975)

Paperwork and the Older Americans Act: Problems of Implementing Accountability. C.L. Estes and Maureen Noble. Report of the Special Committee on Aging, U.S. Senate (Washington, DC: Government Printing Office, June 1973)

"Private Proprietary Homes for Adults: Their Administration, Management, Control, Operation, Supervision, Funding and Quality." An interim Report." (New York, NY: Special Prosecutor for Nursing Homes, Health and Social Services, 1977)

Professional Obligations and Approaches to the Aged. Arthur Schwartz and Ivan Mensh, eds. (Springfield, IL: C.C. Thomas, 1974)

"Proposal for Continual Funding as a State-Wide Senior Citizens' Back-Up Center, or, in the Alternative, as a National Senior Citizens Back-Up Center," California Legal Assistance Senior Citizens Project, Los Angeles.

Report of the Commission. The Moreland Act Commission (Nursing Homes). (Albany, NY: Moreland Act Commission, 1976). Hearings from October 1975-March 1976.

Residential Work with the Elderly. C. Paul Brearley (Boston, MA: Routeledge & Kegan Paul, 1977).

The Emerging Aging Network: Directory of State and Area Agencies, Select Committee on Aging, U.S. House of Representatives, Comm. Publ. No. 95-166 (Washington, D. C.: Government Printing Office, November 1978).

128

ADVOCACY

A Public Citizen's Action Manual, Donald K. Ross (New York, NY: Grossman Publishers, 1973).

Advocacy and Age: Issues, Experience, Strategy, Paul Kraschner, ed. (Los Altos, CA: Geron X, 1976).

Advocacy in the Field of Aging. U.S. Human Resources Corporation, CF 000-042, AoA Contract, HEW-OS-74-237, 1975. Available from the National Clearinghouse on Aging, Parklawn Drive, Rockville, Maryland 20852.

Advocacy Spectrum (Manual for Law for Non-Lawyers Course) National Public Law Training Center, Washington, D.C., 1979.

Due Process - Concentrated Training Module (Washington, D.C.: National Paralegal Institute, 1977).

Education for Critical Consciousness, Paulo Freire (New York, NY: The Seabury Press, 1973).

For the People: A Consumer Action Handbook, Joanne Manning Anderson (Reading, PA: Addison-Wesley, 1977).

Media Portrayal of the Elderly, Hearing before the Select Committee on Aging, U.S. House of Representatives, Ninety-Sixth Congress, Second Session, April 26, 1980. Committee publication 96-231.

"Nader Recruits Retirees to Effect Social Changes," Harvest Years, Vol. 12, April 1972.

Nursing Homes - A Citizen's Action Guide. Linda Horn and Elma Greisel (Boston, MA: Beacon Press, 1977).

"Old Age Associations in National Politics," Henry J. Pratt, Annals of the American Academy of Political and Social Sciences, Vol. 415, September 1974. (Philadelphia, PA: American Academy of Political and Social Sciences, 1974).

Old Age: The Last Segregation (Ralph Nader's study group report on nursing homes). Claire Townsend, Project Director (New York, NY: Grossman Publishers, 1971).

Old is not a Four-Letter Word! Jean B. Abernathy (Nashville, TN: Abington Press, 1975.

"Ombudsman or Citizen Defender: A Modern Institution" Roy Paul and Thurston Sellin. Annals of American Academy of Political and Social Sciences, Vol. 377, 1968.

Pedagogy of the Oppressed. Paulo Freire (N.Y.: The Seabury Press, 1968)

Releasing the Potential of the Older Volunteer. Ethel Percy Andrus Gerontology Center Volunteer Project (Los Angeles, CA.: Office of Publishing and Media Projects, 1976).

Research, Planning & Action For The Elderly. Donald Kent, et al. (N.Y.: Herman Science Press, 1972)

Rights of the Elderly and Retired. William Wishard (San Francisco: Cragmont Publications, 1978)

Rules For Radicals. Saul Alinsky (N.Y.: Vintage Books 1972)

Senior Citizens' Manual: Summary of Rights and Helpful Advice. Delaware County Legal Assistance Association, Inc., 410 Welsh St., Chester, PA.

Senior Power: Growing Old Rebelliously. Paul Kleyman (San Francisco: Cragmont Publications, 1974)

"Social Protection and the Over-75's: What Are The Problems?", Pierre Laroque, International Social Security Review, Vol. 31, No. 3, 1978

"Ten Rules of Legislative Advocacy", David B. Frohnmayer. American Humane, July 1978

The Gray Lobby. Henry J. Pratt (Chicago, Ill.: University of Chicago Press, 1976)

The Law and Aging Manual, Legal Research and Services For The Elderly, National Council of Senior Citizens, 1511 K St., Washington, D.C., 1976

The Other Generation: The New Power of Older People. Rochelle Jones (Englewood Cliffs: Prentice Hall,1977)

The Pursuit of Dignity: New Living Alternative for the Elderly. Bert Kruger Smith (Boston, Beacon Press 1977)

The Rights of Americans: What They Are And What They Should Be, Norman Dorsen, ed. (N.Y.: Vantage Books, 1971)

The Rights of Hospital Patients. ACLU Handbook. George Annas (N.Y.: Avon Books, 1975)

The Rights of Older Persons. ACLU Handbook, Robert Brown, with Clifford Allo, Alan Freeman and Gordon Netzorg (N.Y.: Avon Books, 1979)

The Rights Of The Poor. ACLU Handbook. Sylvia Law (N.Y.: Avon Books 1974)

The Santa Cruz Story: Older People Serving Older People In A Legal Setting. National Paralegal Institute 2000 P St., N.W. Washington, D.C.

The Screwing of the Average Man. David Hapsgood (N.Y.: Bantam Books, 1974)

The Silver Lobby: A Guide to Advocacy for Older Persons, Clinton W. Hess and Paul A. Kerschner, (Los Angeles, CA. Ethel Percy Andrus Gerontology Center, 1978)

"When Nursing Home Patients Complain: The Ombudsman of the Patient Advocate", J.J. Reagan. Georgetown Law Journal 65: 691 (Fall 1977)

Whistle Blowing. Ralph Nader, Peter J. Petkas and Kate Blackwell, eds. (N.Y.: Grossman Publishing, 1972)

COMPARATIVE

A Healthy State. Victor W. Sidel and Ruth Sidel
(N.Y.: Pantheon Books, 1977)

Aging in India. Kirpal Singh Sandan (Calcutta:
Minerva Associates 1975)

Aging in Western Societies. Ernest Watson Burgess
(Chicago, Ill.: University, Chicago, 1960)

"Flexible Retirement: Will Sweden Make It Work?"
Harriet Miller, Dynamic Maturity (Washington, D.C.:
American Association of Retired Persons) March 1976

Geriatric Care In Advanced Societies. J. C. Brockle-
hurst (Baltimore, Md.: University Park Press, 1975)

Good Company: A Study of Nyakyusa Age Villages.
Monica Hunter Wilson (Boston: Beacon Press, 1963)

Homes For The Aged: Supervision and Standard (A Re-
port Of The Legal Situation in European Countries).
Ernest Noam (Translated by John Monks). U.S. Depart
ment of Health, Education and Welfare, Office of
Human Development, Administration on Aging (Washington
D.C.; Government Printing Office, 1975)

Housing The Aged in Western Countries. Glenn H. Beyer
and F.H.J. Nierstrasz (Amsterdam, N.Y.: Elsevier
Publishing Co., 1967)

Housing The Elderly. Department of The Environment,
Great Britain, (Lancaster, England: M.T.P. Construction, 1974)

Old Age In European Society: The Case of France. Peter
Stearns (N.Y.: Holmes & Meier, 1976)

"Old Age Security Abroad: The Background of Titles II
and VIII of the Social Security Act", Barbara Nachrieb
Armstrong, in Cases and Materials on Employment Relations, Wex Malone, Marius Plant and Joseph Little, eds.
(St. Paul, Minnesota: West Publishing Co. 1977)

Old People In Three Industrial Societies. E. Shanas,
Et al. (N.Y.: Atherton Press, 1968)

Ombudsman and Others: Protection in Nine Countries.
Walter Gellhorn (Cambridge, Ma.: Harvard University
Press, 1966)

Ombudsmen Around The World: A Comparative Chart, 2nd
Edition, Kent M. Weeks (Berkeley, Ca.: Institute of
Governmental Studies, University of California at
Berkeley, 1978)

Protecting Social Security Beneficiary Earnings: The
Foreign Experience. Elizabeth Kreitler Kirkpatrick.
U. S. Department of Health, Education and Welfare,
Social Security Administration, HEW Publ. No. 77-11850
(Washington, D.C.: Government Printing Office, 1977)

Social Security. Robert J. Myers (Homewood, Ill.:
Robert D. Irwin, Inc., 1975) Esp., Chapter 17,
"Foreign Social Security Systems"

Social Services In International Perspective. Alfred
J. Kahn and Sheila B. Kamerman. U.S. Dept. of Health,
Education and Welfare, Social and Rehabilitative Ser-
vices, Office of Planning, Research and Evaluation.
(SRS) 76-05704 (Washington, D.C.: Government Print-
ing Office, 1976)

The Graying Of Nations: Implications. Hearing Before
The Special Committee on Aging, United States Senate.
No. 99-586 (Washington, D.C.: Government Printing
Office, 1978)

The Honorable Elders: A Cross-Cultural Analysis of
Aging in Japan. Erdman Ballagh Palmore (Durham,N.C.:
Duke University Press, 1975)

The Old Ones In Mexico. Robert Coles (Albuquerque,
N.M: University of New Mexico, 1973)

The Last Refuge, A Survey of Residential Institutions
and Homes For The Aged In England and Wales. Peter
Townsend (London: Routledge & Kegan Paul, 1962)

CRIME

Crime and the Elderly. Jack Goldsmith and Sharon
Goldsmith (Lexington, MA. Lexington Book, 1976)

"Crime and the Elderly: What Your Community Can Do."
Hearing Before the Special Committee on Aging, U.S.
Senate, June 23, 1980 (1981) (96th Congress, 2nd
session)

Crime Prevention Handbook. National Institute of Law
Enforcement and Criminal Justice, LEAA. U. S. Department of Justice, January 1977

Elder Abuse: The Hidden Problem:, A Briefing By The
Select Committee on Aging, U. S. House of Representa-
tives, 96th Congress, 2nd session, June 23, 1979,
Comm. Publ. No. 96-220 (Washington,D.C. Government
Printing Office, 1980) Joint Hearing June 11, 1980,
Report, April 3, 1981, Comm. Publ. 97-277

Elder Abuse: U. S. Department of Health & Human Services, AoA, Developed Under Contract H.E.W. 105-79-
3010 (May, 1980)

"Granny Bashing", Suzanne K. Steinmetz. Human Behavior 8:48, April, 1979

"Grandma Helps Fight Crime", Reprinted from Police
Chief, Vol. XLIV, No. 2, February 1977

"In Search of Security: A National Perspective on
Elderly Crime Victimization", Report by the Sub-
committeee on Housing and Consumer Interest of the
Select Committee on Aging, April, 1977 (1977) (95th
Congress, 1st session,) Comm. Publ. No. 95-87

"Police Service Delivery to Elderly," Steven Schack
and Robert S. Frank, Annals of American Academy of
Political and Social Sciences July 1978 (Philadelphia
PA. AAPSS)

Research Into Crimes Against The Elderly (Part I),
Hearing Before The Select Committee on Aging, U. S.
House of Representatives, January 31, 1978. Comm. Publ.
No. 95-122 (Washington, D.C.: Government Printing
Office, 1978)

"Step-Up In Fight On Crimes Against The Elderly", U. S. News and World Report, June 13, 1977

"The Elderly Prisoners of Fear", Time, November 29, 1976

"The Proposed Fiscal 1982 Budget: What It Means For Older Americans", An Information Paper Prepared By The Staff of the Special Committee on Aging, U. S. Senate, February 1980 (1981) (96th Congress, 1st session)

"Victim Compensation and the Elderly: Policy and Administrative Issues", A Report by the Criminal Justice and the Elderly Program, Legal Research and Services for the Elderly, of the National Council of Senior Citizens to the Select Committee on Aging, U. S. House of Representatives, January 1979 (1979) (96th Congress, 1st session) Comm. Publ. No. 96-179

"Violent Crime Against the Elderly", A Briefing by the Select Committee on Aging, U. S. House of Representatives, June 1978 (1978) (95th Congress, 2nd session) Comm. Publ. No. 95-146

ECONOMIC

A Shoppers's Guide to Life and Health Insurance for
Senior Citizens, Division of Consumer Services, Department of Insurance, Trenton, New Jersey, 1980

A Study of the Effects of Rising Energy Prices on the
Low and Moderate Income Elderly: Final Report.
(Washington, D. C. : U. S. Federal Energy Administration)

Aging in New Jersey: An Economic Analysis. Gladys
B. Ellenbogen (Upper Montclair, N.J.: Montclair State
College, 1971)

"Comment: Tax Benefit for the Elderly: A Need for
Revision," 1969 Utah Law Review 84 (January 1969)

Consumers Guide to Federal Publications, Available
through Government Printing Office, Washington, D.C.
20402 (Superintendent of Documents)

Consumer Information Catalog, Consumer Information
Center, Pueblo, Colorado (1980)

Economic Problems of Retirement. George B. Hurff, ed.
A Report on the 4th Annual Southern Conference on
Gerontology held at University of Florida, January
27-28, 1954 (Gainesville, Fla.: University of Florida
1954)

Economics of a Stationary Population: Implication for
Older Americans, Juanita Kreps, et al. National
Science Foundation, RA-770024 (Washington: Government
Printing Office, 1977)

"Energy Assistance Programs and Pricing Policies in
the 50 States to Benefit Elderly, Disabled or Low-
Income Households," A Working Paper prepared for
use by the Special Committee on Aging, United States
Senate, October, 1979 (1979) (96th Congress, 1st
session)

"Energy Equity and the Elderly in the 80's"Hearing
Before the Special Committee on Aging, United States
Senate, October 28, 1980 (1981) (96th Congress, 2nd
session).

"How Old is Old? The Effects of Aging on Learning and
Working", Hearing before the Special Committee on
Aging, U. S. Senate (96th Congress, 2nd session),
Washington,D.C. Government Publication Office, 1980)
April 30, 1980.

"Inflation and New York's Elderly", Hearing Before The
Subcommittee on Retirement Income and Employment of
the Select Committee on Aging, House of Representatives, January 10,1980 (1980) (96th Congress, 2nd
session) Comm. Pub. No. 96-229

Pensions, Inflation and Growth: A Comparative Study
of the Elderly in the Welfare State. Thomas Wilson
(London, Heinemann Educational, 1974)

Property Tax Relief Programs for the Elderly Prepared by Abt Associates, Inc. (Washington,D.C.: U.S.
Department of Housing and Urban Development, Office
of Public Development and Research, 1975)

"Protecting Older Americans Against Overpayment of
Income Taxes", Checklist of Itemized Deductions,
Prepared by Staff of Special Committee on Aging,U.S.
Senate, 1979

"Social Security:What Changes Are Necessary?" Hearing
Before the Special Committee on Aging, U.S.Senate,
December 4, 1980, (1981) (96th Congress, 2nd session)

State Tax Relief for the Elderly: Determining the
Costs (Lexington, Ky.; Council of State Governments,
1976)

"Summary of Recommendations and Surveys on Social
Security and Pension Policies", An Information Paper
Prepared for the Special Committee on Aging, U. S.
Senate by the Congressional Research Service of the
Library of Congress, October, 1980 (1980) (96th
Congress, 2nd session)

Tax Counseling for the Elderly Report to Accompany
H.R. 3553, Report No. 95-1667 (Washington,D.C., U.S.,
Government Printing Office, 1978)

The Economics of Aging - James Schulz (Belmont, CA.
Wadsworth, Publ., 1980)

"The Impact of the Rising Costs of Energy, Transportation, Health, Housing, and Other Necessities on Senior Citizens", Hearings before the Subcommittee on
aging, House of Representatives, September 6 &8,1980
(1981) (96th Congress, 2nd session)

The Measurement of Economic Welfare: Its Application
to Aged. M. Moon, Ed. (N.Y.: Academic Press, 1977)

"Why Are Older Consumers So Susceptible." Robert N.
Butler, Gerontologist, Vol. 23, December 1968: 83-
88.

"Work After 65: Options for the 80's," Hearing before
the Special Committe on Aging U. S. Senate, 96th
congress, 2nd session, July 9, 1980 (Washington,D.C.:
Government Printing Office, 1980)

EDUCATION

Alternatives For Later Life and Learning - Some Programs Designed for Older Persons at State Colleges and Universities. (Washington,D.C.: American Association of State Colleges and Universities, 1974)

Creativity Research and its Implications for Adult Education. Jane C. Zahn, (Brookline, MA. Center for the Study of Liberal Education for Adults at Boston University, 1966)

Educating Older People. Second Edition, Mary Frances Cleugh (London: Tavistock Pub., 1970) Dist. in U. S. by Barnes and Noble, N.Y.

Education for Senior Adults. Andrew Hendrickson and George F. Aker (Tallahassee, FL: Dept. of Adult Education, Florida State University, 1969)

"Fountain of Growth: Program for the Elderly at the University of San Diego", Human Services 8:58, May, 1979

"Migration, Age and Education". Abe Schwartz: Journal of Political Economy, Vol. 84 (August 1976)

Seminars for Seniors: An Experiment in Educational Television for the Elderly. Martin McGowin, Jr. and Betty McRoberts (St. Paul: Twin City Area Educational TV Corp.)

Senior Citizen Higher Education Opportunity Act.Hearings, Comm. on Education and Labor, U. S. House of Representatives 3542, June 11, 1977 (Washington D.C.; U. S. Government Printing Office, 1977)

EMPLOYMENT

Age Discrimination In Employment. William Kundit
(N.Y.: American Management Associates, 1978)

"Age Discrimination: Involuntary Retirement", 66
Georgetown Law Review 173(October, 1977)

"An Evaluation of Mandatory Retirement", Harrison J.
Givens, Jr., Annals of American Academy of Political
And Social Sciences, Vol. 438, July 1978 (Philadel-
phia, PA: AAPSS, 1978)

Avocational And Employment Needs of Retired Persons.
Hearing of Select Committee on Aging, U. S. House of
Representatives, held in Hackettstown, N.J., Feb. 11,
1978. Comm. Publ. 95-162 (Washington, D.C.: Government Printing Office, 1978)

Cases and Issues In Age Discrimination. Employee
Relations Law Journal. Vol 3, Winter 1978. Congressional Research Service - LRS 78-3470

Employment, Income And Retirement Problems of the
Aged, Juanita M. Kreps, ed. (Durham, NC. Duke University Press, 1963)

Employment Opportunities For Men And Women After 60.
Juvenal Londono Angel (N.Y.: World Trade Academy
Press, 1969)

Federal Age Discrimination In Employment Law. Charles
Edelman and Ilene Siegler (Charlottesville, VA:
Michie Company, 1978)

Impact Of The Age Discrimination In Employment Act of
1967. Hearings of the Subcommittee on Retirement Income and Employment of Select Committee on Aging,
House of Representatives, Held on February 10, 18,25
1976. (Washington, D.C.: Government Printing Office
1976)

"Issues of Mandatory Retirement". Harold Shephard.
Annals of American Academy of Political and Social
Sciences, July 1978

"Mandatory Retirement And The ADEA", 4 Ohio Northern
Reporter 748 (October 1977) T. J. Reed

"Mandatory Retirement" G. Drucker. 5 Western State
University L.R. 1 (Fall 1977)

Public Policy And The Future Of Work And Retirement
Hearings of Subcommittee on Retirement Income and
Employment and Subcommittee on Human Services, Se-
lect Committee of Aging, U. S. House of Representa-
tives May 3, 1978 Comm. Publ. No. 95-143 (Washington
D.C.: Government Printing Office 1978)

GENERAL

"Age Discrimination in the Selection of Federal Judges", Hearing Before the Select Committee on Aging, House of Representatives, February 13, 1980 (1980) (96th Congress, 2nd Session) Comm. Pub. No. 96-228.

Aging in America, Bart Kruger Smith (Boston, MASS.: Beacon Press, 1973)

Aging in a Changing Society. Ruth E. Albrecht (Gainesville, Florida: University of Florida Press, 1962)

Aging: Prospect and Issues. Richard H. Davis (Los Angeles: Ethel Percy Andrus Gerontology Center, University of Southern California, 1976)

Aging: Scientific Perspectives and Social Issues. D. Woodruff and James Birren, eds. (N.Y.: D. Van Nostrand Co., 1975)

Alternatives to Institutional Care for Older Americans. Eric Pfeiffer, ed. (Durham, NC: Center for Study of Aging and Human Development, Duke University, 1973)

"Americans Over 100", Hearing Before the Select Committee on Aging, House of Representatives, Nov. 14, 1979 (1980) (96th Cong. 1st session) Comm. Publ. No. 96-203

"Can We Invalidate Negative Stereotypes of Aging?" Clark Tibbitts, Gerontologist, Vol. 19, February, 1979)

Developments in Aging: 1978. Part I. A Report of the Special Committee on Aging, United States Senate, Report No. 96-55 (March 30, 1979)

"Domestic Violence Against the Elderly", Hearing before the Subcommittee on Human Services, Select Committee on Aging, House of Representatives, April 21, 1980 (1980) (96th Congress, 2nd session) Comm. Pub. No. 96-233

142

Effective Social Service for Older Americans. Sheldon
S. Tobin, Steven M Davidson, and Ann Sack (Michigan
Institute of Gerontology, University of Michigan -
Wayne State University, 1976)

"Families: Aging and Changing", Hearing Before the
Select Committee on Aging, House of Representatives,
November 24, 1980 (1981) (96th Congress, 2nd session)
Comm. Pub. No. 96-275A

Green Winter: Celebrations of Old Age. Elise Maclay.
(N.Y.: Reader's Digest Press, distributed by Crowell
1977)

Growing Old In America. David Hacker Fisher (London:
Oxford University Press, 1977)

Growing Old in America. Beth Hess (Edison, N.J.:
Transaction Books, 1976)

Growing Old In the Country of the Young. Charles H.
Percy (N.Y.: McGraw-Hill Co., 1973)

Handbook of Aging Series (Three Volumes). James
Birren (N.Y.: Van Nostrand Reinhold Co., 1977)

Independent Living for Older People, Proceedings,
Southern Conference on Gerontology. Published under
the auspices of the Center for Gerontological Studies and Programs, University of Florida.(Gainesville,
Florida: Unversity of Florida Press, 1972)

Introduction to Gerontology. Arthur N. Schwartz and
James A. Paterson (N.Y.: Holt, Rinehart & Winston Co.
1979)

Inventory of Federal Statistical Programs Relating to
Older Persons (Department of Health, Education and
Welfare) DHEW Publ. No.(01105) 79-20291 (January 1979)

Legislation in the 95th Congress Relating to Aging.
Evelyn Tager. Congressional Research Service. HD
7106A, Rep. No. 78-230 EPW (November 21, 1978)

Old Age in a New Land, W. Andrew Achenbaum (Baltimore,
MD. Johns Hopkins Unversity Press, 1979)

"Older Americans Act: A Staff Summary" by the Select
Committee on Aging, U. S. House of Representatives,
Revised July 1979 (1979) (96th congress, 1st session)
Comm. Publ. No. 96-185

Older Americans Handbook. Craig T. Norbach (N.Y.:
Van Nostrand Reinhold Co., 1977)

On Growing Old: A Study of Aging. Council of State
Governments (Lexington, Ky.: Council of State Governments, 1973)

Over 55 Is Not Illegal. Frances Tenenbaum (Boston:
Houghton Mifflin, Co., 1979)

"Regulations to Implement the Comprehensive Older
Americans Act Amendments of 1978", Joint Hearing
Before the Special Committee on Aging, United States
Senate.

Socialization to Old Age. Irving Rosow (Los Angeles
CA: University of California, Press Ltd., 1974)

Social Services and Aged. Joseph Davenport and Judith
Davenport (Washington: University Press, 1976)

Social Welfare of the Aging. Proceedings, Vol. II,
Jerome Kaplan and G. J. Aldridge, Eds. (Aging in the
World Series) (N.Y.: Columbia University Press, 1962)

The Billion $ Swindle: Frauds Against the Elderly.
Amram Ducovny (N.Y.: Fleet Press Corporation, 1969)

"The Abuse of the Urban Aged", James Birren, Psychology Today, March 1970

The Coming of Age. Simone de Beauvoir (Translated by
Patrick O'Brien) (N.Y.: Putnam Books, 1972)

The Myth and Reality of Aging in America. Louis Harris
and Associates Inc. (National Council on Aging, Inc.
July, 1976)

The New Old: Struggling for Decent Aging. Ronald
Gross and Sylvia Seidman, eds. (Garden City, N.Y.:
Anchor Press, 1979)

The Social Challenge of Aging. David Hobman, Ed. (N.Y.: St. Martin's Press, 1978)

To Find The Way To Opportunities and Service For Older Americans, Department of Health, Education and Welfare, Office of Human Development, Administration on Aging. DHEW Publ. No. 75-20807 (AoA)

When Your Parents Grow Old. Jane Otten and Florence D. Shelley (N.Y.: New Amsterdam Library, 1976)

Why Survive? Being Old in America. Robert N. Butler (N.Y.: Harper & Row, 1975)

Working With Older People: A Guide to Practice. Vol. I: The Knowledge Base. Dept. of HEW, Health Care Financing Administration, Health Standards and Quality Bureau, Parklawn Building, 5600 Fishers' Lane Rockville, MD.

You and Your Aging Parent, Barbara Silverstone and Helen Kandel Hyman (N.Y.: Pantheon Books, 1976)

HEALTH

A Healthy State. Victor W. Sidel and Ruth Sidel.(N.Y.:
Pantheon Books, 1977)

"Drug Abuse in Nursing Homes" Hearing Before The Select Committee on Aging, House of Representatives,June
25, 1980 (1980) (96th Congress, 2nd session) Comm.
Pub. No. 96-244

Federalized Health Care For The Aged? A Critical Symposium. (Chicago, Ill.: American Medical Association
1963)

"Home Care Services For Older Americans: Planning
For The Future" Hearings Before the Special Committee
on Aging, U. S. Senate, May 7 and 21, 1979 (1979)
(96th Congress, 1st session)

Hospital Insurance Benefits: A Programmed Learning
Text. U. S. Department of Health, Education and Welfare, Social Security Administration (BHI Pub.No.003,
1-77)

"Long Term Health Care for The Aged", C.O. Murray,
39 Albany Law Review 617 (1975)

Meal System For the Elderly: Policy Research Project
Lyndon Baines Johnson School For Public Affairs
(Austin, Texas: Lyndon B. Johnson School For Public
Affairs, 1977)

Medicare And The American Rhetoric of Reconciliation.
Max Skidmore (Alabama: University of Alabama Press,
1970)

Medicare In A Changing Society. Lawrence Corey,
Steven E. Waltman and Michael F. Epstein (St. Louis,
Mo.: C. V. Mosby & Co. 1977) Especially, Chapter 5,
"The Elderly And Disease - Medicare And Medicaid -
Help and Hindrance", Agnes V. Brewster

National Health Insurance. Karen Davis (Washington,
D.C.: Brookings Institute, 1975)

146

<u>Nursing Home Administration.</u> Stephen M. Schneeweiss
and Stanley W. Davis (Baltimore, Md.: University Park
Press, 1974)

<u>Nursing Homes in the 70's.</u> David Lebenbom (N.Y.:
Practicing Law Institute, 1973)

<u>Nutrition And Aging.</u> Ruth Weg. (Los Altos, Ca.: Geron
X Publishing, 1978)

"Nutrition and Aging: A Monograph for Practitioners",
M. Loeb and S. Howell, eds. <u>Gerontologist,</u> 1969,9:3

<u>Prognosis Negative: Crisis In Health Care System.</u>
David Kotelchuk, ed. (N.Y.: Vintage Books, 1976)
especially, "The Politics of Health Care: What Is It
Costing You?", Godfrey Hodgson

<u>Tender Loving Greed.</u> Mary Adelaide Mendelsohn (N.Y.:
Vintage Books, 1975)

<u>The Great American Medicine Show.</u> Spencer Klaw (N.Y.:
Penguin Books, 1976) Especially, Chapter 11, "The
Trouble With Medicare and Medicaid"

<u>The Nursing Home Law Handbook.</u> National Senior Citi-
zens' Law Center, 1709 West 8th Street, Los Angeles,
Cal., 1975

<u>The Nation's Use of Health Resources.</u> Charles H.
Croner. U. S. National Center For Health Statistics,
Division Of Health Resources Utilization Statistics,
DHEW Publ. No. (HRA) 77-1240 (Washington,D.C.: Govern-
ment Printing Office, 1976)

HOUSING

Areawide Planning for Independent Living for Older
People. Carter Osterbinder (Gainesville,FL.: University of Florida Press, 1973)

Beyond Shelter: A Study Of National Housing Act Fin-
anced Housing For The Elderly. Michael J. Audain
(Ottawa, Canada: Canadian Council on Social Development, 1973)

Congregate Housing for Older People, Edited by Wilma
T. Donahue, Marie McGuire Thompson and D. J. Curren
for U. S. Department of Health, Education and Welfare
Office of Human Development, Administration on Aging
(1977) DHEW Pub. No. (OHD) 77-20284

Housing and Community Developments Amendments of 1978
Report of Committee on Banking, Finance & Urban Affairs, United States House of Representatives, Report
No. 95-1161 (Washington, D.C:Government Printing Office, 1978)

Housing and Social Services For The Elderly: Social
Policy Trends. Elizabeth Huttman (N.Y.: Praeger
Publishers, 1977)

"Housing For The Elderly: Constitutional Limitations
and Our Obligations" 35 Florida State University Law
Review 423 (Summer 1977)

Housing For The Elderly: Evaluation Of Effectiveness
Of Congregate Projects. Irene Malzernow, et al.
(Boulder, Colorado: Westview Publ., 1978)

Housing For The Elderly: The Development And Design
Process. Isaac Green et al. (N.Y.: Van Nostrand & Co.
1975)

Housing In Retirement: Some Pointers For Social Policy (N.Y.: International Publications Service, 1974)

Housing Law For Non-Lawyers. National Paralegal Institute, National Public Law Training Center, 2000
P. Street, N.W. Washington, D. C., 1979

Housing The Aged. Conference on Aging at the University
of Michigan, 1952. Wilma Donahue, ed. Ann Arbor: University of Michigan Press, 1954

Housing The Elderly. Pete J. Horobin (Boston: Herman
Publishing, 1974)

Impact of Federal Housing Programs on the Elderly.
Susan Dovvall (rev. by Susan Vanhorenbeck Congress-
ional Research Service. Publication No. CRS 78-66E
March 18, 1978).

Loners, Losers and Lovers: Elderly Tenants In A Slum
Hotel. Joyce Stephens (Seattle, Washington: University
of Washington 1976)

Planning and Managing Housing for the Elderly. Mary
Powell Lawton (N.Y.: Wiley Interscience, 1975)

"Retirement Communities: Nature of Enforceability of
Residential Segregation by Age", M. Doyle. 76 Michigan
Law Review 64 (Nov. 1977)

"Unseen Community: Understanding The Older Hostel
Dweller". J. K. Eckert. Aging 291: 28-35 (January 1979)

Urban Problems and Prospects. Anthony Downs (Chicago,
Ill.: Markham Publications, 1971)

INCOME

Age and Poverty, William Withers. (Woodbury, N.Y.:
Barron's Educational Series, 1978)

Employment, Income and Retirement: Problems of Aging
Juanita M. Kreps, ed. (Durham, N.C.: Duke University
Press, 1963)

"Four Issues in Income Mainteance for the Aged during the 1970's", Joseph Krislow, Social Service Re-
View, Vol. 42, September 1968: 335-343

Fundamentals of Private Pensions. Don M. McGill.
(Homewood, Ill.: Richard D. Irwin, Inc., 1975)

Income and Poverty Among the Elderly. Donald G. Fowles
Department of Health, Education and Welfare, Office
of Human Development, Administration on Aging. DHEW
Publ. No. 77-20286 (Washington, D.C.: Government
Printing Office, 1975)

Pensions and Profit Sharing. Herman C. Biegel, et al.
Washington, D.C.: BNA Inc. 1956

Providing Adequate Retirement Income: Pension Reform
In the U.S. and Abroad. James Schulz et al. (Hanover,
N.H.: University Press of New England, 1974

Senior Citizens: A Guide To Entitled Benefits. Mary
J. Tripp (Redwood City, CA.: Whole Oak Publishing
Co., 1977)

Social Security: Today and Tomorrow. Robert M. Ball
(N.Y.: Columbia University Press, 1978)

The Aged and Social Security: Social Security Developments And Planning And Protection Of The Aged. Report of the International Labor Org., Commission of
Social Development, United Nations Economic and
Social Council E/CN. 5/533, September 17, 1976

The Keogh Retirement Plan; A Tax Shelter For The Self-Employed, A Sales Talk (Indianapolis, Indiana: Research & Review Service of America, 1974)

"The Unfinished Task of Private Pension Reform", Bruce K. Miller and Neal S. Dudovitz, Trial, Vol. 13, May 1977

You and Your Pension. Ralph Nader and Kate Blackwell (N.Y.: Grossman Publishing, 1973)

LEGAL

Community Legal Education For Senior Citizens (Instruct-
or's Guide) National Paralegal Institute, 1714 Stockton
Street, San Francisco, California, 94133

"Florida's Life Care Law: Revitilizing A Dormant
Statute To Protect The Elderly". University of Florida
Law Review, 1976

Improving Legal Representation For Older Americans,
Hearings Before the Special Committee on Aging, U.S.
Senate; June 14, 1974 (Washington, D.C.: Government
Printing Office, 1974); August 30, 1976, September
28 & 29, 1976 (Washington, D.C.: Government Printing
Office, 1977)

"Introduction: Themes and Issues on Gerontology and
Law," Martin Levine, Law Library Journal, Vol. 73.
pp, 259-235

Justice and Older Americans. Marlene Rifai, ed.
(Lexington, MA: Lexington Books, 1977)

Legal Problems Of The Poor: Cases and Materials.
Arthur Berney, et al., eds. (Boston: Little Brown &
Co., 1975) Especially, Part I, Housing and Part IV,
Consumer Protection

"On Being Imposed Upon By Artful and Designing Persons:
The California Experience With Involuntary Placement",
C.J. Alexander. 14 San Diego Law Review 108

Poverty Law Reporter - Loose-leaf Service, Updated
Regularly. Available from Commerce Clearinghouse
Chicago, Illinois. The Poverty Law Reporter is a
two volume set and items of particular interest are
in income, welfare, consumer protection, housing,
landlord/tenant law.

REPORT: Program For Legal Education For The Elderly.
Legal Assistance Foundation of Chicago, 64 E. Jackson
Blvd., Chicago, Ill.

Social Work And Law. Donald Brieland and John Lemmon (St. Louis, Minn.: West Publishing Co., 1977) Especially, Chapter 16, "Legal Problems of Aged" and Chapter 19, "Poverty and Income Maintenance"

SYMPOSIUM: Aged in America. 10 Trial 130 (April 1974) and 13 Trial 12 (May 1977), (Legal Problems Confronting The Elderly.)

SYMPOSIUM: Law And The Aged. 17 Arizona Law Review 267 (1975)

SYMPOSIUM: Legal Problems Of The Elderly. 9 Connecticut Law Review 425 (Spring 1977)

The Law Of The Elderly. Jonathan Weiss, ed. (N.Y.: Practicing Law Institute, 1977)

"The Senior Citizen's Project of California Rural Legal Assistance: An Action Arm of the National Senior Citizen's Law Center". Wanda Collins, Jean Flanagan and Terrence Donnelley. Clearinghouse Review, Vol. 6, August/September 1972

MINORITIES

Comprehensive Service Delivery Systems for the Minority Aging (Vol. IV, Proceedings of the Institute on Minority Aging), E. Percil Stanford, ed. (San Diego: Campanile Press, San Diego State University, 1978)

"Life After 65", Nancy Hicks, Black Enterprise, May 1977

Minority Aging and the Legislative Process. E. Percil Stanford, ed. (San Diego Center on Aging, Proceedings of the Third Institute of Minority Aging, 1977)

"Minority Elders: Victims of Double Discrimination in Public and Private Benefit Plans," Machael Gilfix, DePaul Law Review, Vol. 27, December, 1978, Pp. 383-405.

National Health Policy and the Underserved: Ethnic Minorities, Women, and the Elderly. Jerry Weaver (St. Louis, Missouri: C.V. Mosby Co., 1978)

"NCBA, Black Aged & Policitics", Jacquelyne Johnson Jackson, Annals of the American Academy of Political and Social Sciences, Vol. 415, September 1974

Older Americans (Statistical Report): Social, Economic and Health Characteristics of Older American Indians. Blanch Williams. U. S. Department of Health, Education and Welfare, Office of Human Development, Administration on Aging. Publication No. (OHDS) 78-20289 (June 1978)

The Elder American Indian. Frank Dukepoo. (San Diego: Campanile Press, 1978)

The Elder Black. E. Percil Stanford. (San Diego: Campanile Press, 1978)

The Elder Latino. Ramon Valle and Lydia Mendoza. (San Diego: Campanile Press, 1978)

The Elder Pilipino. Roberta Peterson (San Diego: Campanile Press, 1978)

The Multiple Hazards of Age and Race: The Situation
of Aged Blacks in the United States. Report of Special
Committee on Aging, United States Senate, Report No.
92-450 (Washington, D.C.: Government Printing Office,
1971)

"The Needs of the Minority Elderly," Hearing Before
the Select Committee on Aging, House of Representatives, March 29, 1978 (1978) (95th Congress, 2nd
session) Comm. Publ. No. 95-155

The Negro Aged: A Minority Within A Minority. Thomas
F. Pettigrew. (Trenton, N.J.: Department of Community
Affairs, Division on Aging, 1969)

The Spanish-Speaking Elderly Poor. A Report to the
Office on Economic Opportunity, Part I (San Francisco.
CA.: Human Resources Corporation, April 1, 1973)

The Urban Aged: Race and Medical Care. Herbert Ashley
Weeks and Benjamin J. Darsky (Ann Arbor, Mich.: University of Michigan, School of Health, 1968)

The Urban Elderly Poor; Racial and Bureaucratic Conflict.
Richard S. Sterne, et al., eds. (Lexington, MA.: Lexington Books, 1974)

"Why A National Caucus on the Black Aged?" Cynthia Coiro,
Harvest Years, Vol. 11, November 1971.

PHYSICAL DISABILITY

An Introduction to Working With The Aging Person Who
Is Visually Handicapped. American Foundation For
the Blind (N.Y.: American Foundation For the Blind,
1972)

"Chemical Time-Bomb: Drug Misuse By The Elderly", J.
R. Solomon, Contemporary Drugs 6:231-243 (Summer 1977)

Drugs And The Elderly. Edward S. Brady, A Paper De-
livered At The Ethel Percy Andrus Gerontology Center
University of Southern California, Los Angeles,1975

Drugs And The Elderly: Social And Pharmacological
Issues. David M. Peterson and Frank J. Whittington
and Barbara Payne (Springfield, Ill.; C.C. Thomas
Company, 1979)

Issue Paper on Legal Problems of Elderly and Handicapped, (Research Institute, Legal Services Corporation, Washington, D.C., 1979)

Northeastern Conference On Aging And Visual Impairment, New Haven. Report Available From American Foundation For The Blind, Community Services Division
1972

"Planning for the Physically and Mentally Handicapped"
J. G. Gorman. 11 Institute on Estate Planning 15(1977)

Rehabilitation: A Manual For The Disabled And The Elderly. Gerald C. Hirschberg, Leon Lewis and Dorothy
Thomas (Philadelphia, PA.: Lippincott, 1964)

Vision Impairment Among Older Americans, Hearing before Congress, August 3, 1978 (Washington, D.C. Government Printing Office, 1978)

PUBLIC ASSISTANCE

A National Guide To Government and Foundation Fund-
ing Sources in the Field of Aging. Lilly Cohen and
Marie Oppedisano Rich (Garden City, N.Y.: Adelphi
University Press , 1977)

"Estate Planning and Resource Maximization for the
Elderly Qualifying for Federal Need Based On Assistance." G. B. Speir. Clearing House Review 10,767-
777 (January 1977)

Federal Programs and Assistance Benefiting the Elderly,
Evelyn Tager, Congression Research Service 78-122 EPW
(June 2, 1978) Washington D.C. Government Printing
Office.

Federal Responsibility to the Elderly. Evelyn Tager
and Robert Bostick For Select Committe on Aging,
United States House of Representatives (Washington,
D.C. U. S. Government Printing Office 1976)

"Federalization of Old Age Assistance: Political Impact on the Aged Poor", The Supplemental Social Security Income Program for the Aged, Blind and Disabled.
U. S. Department of Health, Education and Welfare,
Social Security Administration, ORS. Publication No.
(SSA) 75-11851 (Washington, D.C., Government Printing Office, 1974)

Manual on Public Benefit Programs. Legal Counsel for
the Elderly,(1424 16th Street, N.W. Washington, D.C.
1977)

Medicaid, Policy and Politics: A Case Study and Policy Analysis: Eugene Feingold (San Francisco:Chandler
Publishing Company 1966)

"Outreach: Bringing the Eligible into Federal Assistance Programs,"62 Cornell Law Review 1893 (Aug.1977)

Public Benefit and Entitlements. National Paralegal
Institute, National Public Law Training Center, 2000
P Street, N.W.Washington, D.C. 20036

157

Regulating the Poor: The Functions of Public Welfare.
Francis Fox Piven and Richard A. Cloward.(N.Y.:
Vantage Books, 1971)

Social Goals, Social Programs and Aging. (Gainesville,
Fla.: University of Florida Press, 1976)

Social Security In America. Philip Booth (Ann Arbor:
University of Michigan - Wayne State University, Institute of Labor and Industrial Relations, 1973)

Social Security: Promise and Reality. Ricardo
Campbell, (Stanford, Cal,:Hoover
Institution Press, 1977)

The Evolution of Medicare: From Idea to Law. Peter
A. Corning (Washington, D.C.: U. S. Social Security
Administration, Office of Research and Statistics,
1969) Report No. 29

PUBLIC POLICY

"Age Prejudice in America", Alexander Comfort, Social Policy, Nov./Dec. 1976

"Community Services For the Aged", in Social Services in the United States - Policies And Programs. Sheila Kamerman and Alfred Kahn (Philadelphia, PA: Temple University Press, 1976)

Developments In Aging: 1978. A Report of the Special Committee on Aging, U. S. Senate, Pursuant to S. Res. 375, March 6, 1978 and S. Res. 376, March 6, 1978 (U. S. Government Printing Office, 1978)

Extending The Human Life Span: Social Policy and Social Ethics. Report prepared for the National Science Foundation, RANN, Research Applications Directorate Division of Advanced Productivity, Research and Technology. NSF/RA 770123. Bernice Neugarten & Robert Havighurst, eds. (Univ. of Chicago, Commission on Human Development, 1977)

Federal Responsibility To The Elderly. Select Committee on Aging, U. S. House of Representatives, Comm. Publ. No. 95-167 (Washington, D.C.: Government Printing Office, 1979) January 1979

Guide to AOA Programs, HEW/AOA, DHEW Publication No. (OHDS) 80-20176

Impact On The Elderly Of The Fiscal Year 1979 Budget. Select Committee, U. S. House of Representatives, Comm. Publ. No. 95-144 (Washington, D.C.: Government Printing Office, March 2, 1978)

"Interest Group Liberalism And The Politics of Aging." Robert Binstock, Gerontologist, Vol.12, No. 3, Autumn 1972, Part I

Learning Packages In Policy Issues - Nursing Home Care As A Public Policy Issue. Mary Bednarski and Sandra Florczyk (Croton-On-Hudson: Policy Studies Assoc.1978)

"Long Term Policy Issues: Alternatives To Institutional Care", Faye Abdalah, Annals of American Academy of Political and Social Sciences (Philadelphia,
PA: AAPSS) July 1978

National Clearinghouse On Aging: Advocacy in Aging.
Report Prepared by Norman Hodges & Associates, Inc.
(SCAN: Service Center for Aging Information). U. S.
Department HEW, Administration on Aging, June 1975)

Nursing Home Care In The United States: Failure In
Public Policy; Introductory Report. Special Committee
on Aging, U.S. Senate, Sen. Report No.1420 (Washington,
D.C.: Government Printing Office, 1974)

Nursing Homes and Public Policy. William Thomas, Jr.
(Ithaca, N.Y.: Cornell University, 1969)

Old Age and Political Behavior: A Case Study. Philip
Pinner, Frank Selznick and Paul Jacobs (Berkeley,CA.
University of California Press, 1959)

"Old People and Public Policy" Amitzai Etzioni,
Social Policy, November/December 1976)

Older Americans Act: A Staff Summary. Select Committee
on Aging, U.S. House of Representatives.Comm. Publ.
No. 96-185, (Washington, D.C.: Government Printing
Office, 1976, revised July 1979)

Our Needy Aged: A National Problem. Floyd Bond,et al.
Prepared under the auspices of Pomona College, Social
Science Research Center, Claremont,CA.(N.Y.: Holt & Co.
1954)

Political and Economic Aspects of Age As A Special
Issue. Robin Walther and Neal Cutler (Los Angeles
University of Southern California, 1977)

Politics/America. Walter Dean Burnham (N.Y.: D. Van
Nostrand Co., 1973)

Politics of Medicare. Theodore Marmor (Chicago,
Aldine Publ., 1973)

Private Pensions and the Public Interest:A Symposium (Washington, D.C.: American Enterprise Institute for Public Policy Research, 1970)

Progress In Aging: The 95th Congress. A report of the Select Committee on Aging, U.S.H.R. Comm. Publ. No. 95-175, January, 1979

Report of the Interdepartmental Task Force On Information and Referral, U. S. Department of Health & Human Services, AOA, DHHS Publ. No. (OHDS) 81-20096

Research Planning and Action for the Elderly: The Power and Potential of Social Science. Donald Kent, Robert Kastenbaum and Sylva Sherwood (Behavorial Pub. 1972)

Social Policy, Social Programs and the Aging. Bernice L. Neugarten & Robert Havighurst (National Science Foundation, 1976)

"Study of Programs Affecting The Elderly As They Constitute A National Aging Policy", Elizabeth Ann Kutza. Ph.D. Dissertation - University of Chicago, 1977, Available from National Clearinghouse on Aging. CF 000 793. AOA Grant No., 90-A-708.

The Aged And The Need For Surrogate Management. Gerry Alexander and Travis Lewin (Syrace, N.Y.: Syracuse University Press, 1972)

The Aged Population In The United States: 1963 Social Security Survey Of The Aged. Lenore Epstein and Janet H. Murray. Social Security Administration, Office of Research & Statistics. Report No.19, 1967

"The Aging of America: Questions For A Four Generation Society", Joseph Califano, Jr. Annals of the American Academy of Political and Social Sciences 1978

The Politics of Age, Wilma Donahue and Clark Tibbitts, eds. (Ann Arbor, Division of Gerontology, University of Michigan, 1962)

The Whole Person After 60-Issues in Intergovernmental Planning(Lexington,KY,:Council of State Governments, 1977)

<u>Towards A National Policy On Aging</u>. Proceedings of
the 1971 White House Conference on Aging, November 28
December 2, 1971. Department of HEW, Publ. No. (OHD)
74-20912 (1974)

SOCIAL/PSYCHOLOGICAL

Activities Program For Senior Citizens, Harriet U.
Fish (West Nyack, N.Y.: Parker Company, 1971)

"Aging and I.Q.: The Myth Of The Twilight Years",
Paul B. Baltes and K. Warner-Schaie. Psychology Today, (March 1974)

Aging With Honor And Dignity. Minna Field (Springfield
Ill.: C. C. Thomas, 1968)

Creative Aging. Edward Le Roy Bartz (N.Y.:MacMillan
Co., 1963)

Death Anxiety. H. W. Montefiore, Joseph R. Cautela
and Robert N. Butler(N.Y.: MSS Information Corp.1973)

Handbook of Aging and Social Sciences. Robert Binstock and Ethel Shanas (N.Y.:Van Nostrand Reinhold
Co., 1976)

Independent Living For The Handicapped And The Elderly ,
Elizabeth Eckhardt May (Boston:Houghton Mifflin Co.
1974)

"Leisure Activities For Aging", Mary Powell Lawton,
Annals of the American Academy for Political and
Social Sciences, July 1978)

Let's End Isolation! U. S. Department of Health, Education and Welfare, Administration on Aging. DHEW
Publ. No. 129 (AOA)

Loneliness And Social Alienation Of The Elderly. Hearing Before the Subcommittee on Federal, State and Community Services. Select Comm. on Aging, House of Representatives, November 15, 1977. Comm Publ. No. 95-119
(Washington,D.C.: Government Printing Office, 1978)

Love In The Later Years. James A. Peterson and Barbara Payne (N.Y.: Association Press, 1975)

163

Mandatory Retirement: The Social and Human Cost Of
Enforced Idleness. Report of Select Committee on
Aging, House of Representatives, Aug. 1977. Comm.Pub.
No. 95-91 (Washington, D.C.: Government Printing
Office, 1978)

Nobody Ever Died of Old Age. Sharon B. Curtin (Boston
Little Brown & Company, 1972)

On Old Age And Friendship (De Senectude et. DeAmicitia)
Marcus Tillius Cicero. Translated With Introduction
by Frank Copley (Ann Arbor, Mich: University of Mich.
Press, 1976)

Personal Adjustment To Old Age. Ruth Shonle Cavan
(Chicago, Ill.: Science Research Associates, 1949)

Recreational Activity Development For Aging In Homes,
Hospitals And Nursing Homes. Carol Lucas (Springfield,
Ill.: C. C. Thomas, 1978)

Retirement Communities: Case Studies In Social Gerontology. Jerry Jacobs (Springfield, Ill.: C.C.Thomas,
1975)

Retirement Communities: For Adults Only. Catherine
Heitz (Center For Urban Policy Research, 1976)

Sexuality And Aging. Irene Mortenson Burnside, ed.
(Los Angeles: Ethel Percy Andrus Gerontology Center,
University of Southern Califronia, 1975)

Starting A Recreation Program In Institutions For The
Ill Or Handicapped Aged. Morton Thompson (N.Y.: National Recreation Associates, 1960)

The Aged, The Family And The Community. Minna Field
(N.Y.: Columbia University Press, 1972)

The Daily Needs And Interests of Older People.Adelaide
Hoffman, et al. (Springfield, Ill.:C.C.Thomas, 1970)

The Urban Elderly:A Study of Life Satisfaction. For-
rest J. Berghorn,et al. (Montclair,N.J.:Allenheld,
Osmun & Co., 1978)

164

Towards A Theology of Aging: A Special Issue of
Pastoral Psychology. Seward Hiltner, guest ed.
(N.Y.: Human Services Press, 1975)

TRANSPORTATION

Accessibility of the Metropolitan Washington, D.C.
Public Transportation System to the Handicapped
Elderly. Abt Associates, (Cambridge, Mass.:Harvard
University, 1972)

Developing Transportation Services for the Elderly.
David Rachlis, (Washington, D.C.: National Council
on Aging, 1970)

Mass Transportation Assistance to Meet the Needs of
Elderly and Handicapped Persons. Comm. on Public
Works and Transportation, Hearing on H.R. 5010 (Mar.
30 and April 6, 1977) (Washington,D.C.,U. S. Government Printing Office, 1977)

The Disabled and the Elderly: Equal Access to Public
Transportation James J. Raggio, et al. (Washington,
D.C.: President's Committee on Employment of the
Handicapped, 1957)

The Older Americans - Issues in States' Service -
National Council of State Governments, Lexington, KY.
1976 "Providing Transportation for the Elderly"

Transportation and Aging: Selected Issues Edmund J.
Cantilli and June L. Shmelzer - Based on Proceedings
of the Interdisciplinary Workshop on Transportation
and Aging. May 24-26, 1970 (Washington D.C.,U. S.
Government Printing Office, 1971)

Transportation and the Disadvantaged, John Falcochilo
and Edmund Cantili (Lexington, MA: Lexington Books,
1974)

Transportation for Older Americans:A State of the Art
Report. Institute of Public Administration, 1975
(Distributed by National Technical Information Service)

Transportation Services for the Disabled and Elderly.
Richard K. Brail, James W. Hughes and Carol A.Arthur
(New Brunswick, Rutgers University, 1976)

A High Old Time: or, How To Enjoy Being A Woman Over 60. Lavinia Russ (N.Y.: Saturday Review Press, 1972)

"Aging Is A Woman's Issue", Tish Sommers. Response, United Methodist Women, March 1976

Drug Use Among American Women, Old and Young. Lee Harrington Bowker (San Francisco: Rand Associates, 1977)

Legal Issues Affecting The Older Woman In America. National Clearing House for Legal Services, 500 Michigan Avenue, Chicago, Illinois

National Policy Concerns For Older Women. Federal Council On The Aging (Washington, D.C.: Government Printing Office, 1975)

Older Women: A Workshop Guide. National Commission on the Observance of International Women's Year, 1977. Department of State (Washington,D.C.: Government Printing Office, 1977)

Sex Discrimination And The Law. Barbara Babcock, Ann E. Freeman, Eleanor Holmes Norton, Susan C. Ross (Boston: Little Brown & Company, 1975)

"The Compounding Impact Of Age On Sex: Another Dimension Of The Double Standard", Tish Sommers. Civil Rights Digest (A Quarterly Publication of the U. S. Commission on Civil Rights)Fall 1974

"The Status Of Mid-Life Women and Options For Their Future", A report with additional views by the Sub-Committee on Retirement, Incomes and Employment of the Select Committee on Aging, House of Representatives, March, 1980 (1980)(96th Congress, 2nd Session) Comm. Pub. No. 96-215

The Treatment of Women Under Social Security. HEW Task Force, Dept. of Health, Education and Welfare, (Washington, D.C.:Government Printing Office 1974)

Women After 40:The Meaning of the Last Half of Life.
Grace L. Elliott (N.Y.: H. Holt, 1936)

"Women and Retirement Income Programs: Current Issues
of Equity and Advocacy", A report prepared by Congress-
tional Research Service for the Subcommittee on Retirement, Income and Employment of the Select Committee on Aging, House of Representatives, Nov. 1979.

Appendix

GLOBAL PERSPECTIVES ON ADVOCACY AND AGING

Problems associated with aging have been a matter of stated international policy concern at least since 1948. In that year, the United Nations General Assembly adopted the Universal Declaration of Human Rights, referred to as the Magna Carta for humankind. Article 25 of the Declaration asserted the right to security in old age. Likewise, the Declaration of Social Progress and Development, adopted by the General Assembly in 1969, Res. 2542 (XXIV), proclaimed the necessity of protecting the rights and assuring the welfare of the aged.

In a far-reaching resolution, adopted in 1973 under the title of "Question of the Elderly and the Aged ", Res. 3137 (XXVIII), the General Assembly drew the attention of "member states affected by the problem" to the need for short-term and long-term policies and programs for the elderly. Specifically, the Assembly recommended that governments, in formulating such national programs and policies, take appropriate action to:

(a) Develop, as required and in accordance with their national priorities, programmes for the welfare, health and protection of older people, and their retraining in accordance with their needs, including measures aimed at maximizing their economic independence and their social integration with other segments of the population.

(b) Develop progressively social security measures to ensure that the aged, regardless of sex, receive adequate income.

(c) Enhance the contribution of the elderly to social and economic development.

(d) Discourage wherever and whenever the overall situation allows, discriminatory attitudes,

169

policies and measures in employment practices
based exclusively on age.

(e)   Encourage the creation of employment opportunities for the elderly in accordance with
their needs.

(f)   Promote by all possible means the strength-
ening of the family unit.

(g)   Stimulate bilateral and multilateral agree-
ments of cooperation in the field of social
security for the benefit of the aging.

A companion resolution, adopted at the same
General Assembly session, Res. 3138, stressed the
importance of social security program protection
for the elderly.   As a result of this resolution,
the International Labour Organization prepared a
27 page report under the title, "The Aged and Social
Security -- Social Security Developments and Planning
and Protection of the Aged" (United Nations Economic
and Social Council, E/CN. 5/533, 17 September 1976).

Heightened interest in problems regarding aging
led the General Assembly, at its 1978 session, to
determine that a World Assembly on the Elderly would
be held in 1982 " as a forum to launch an international action program aimed at guaranteeing economic and
social security to older persons as well as opportunities to contribute to national development." (Res.
33/52, adopted December 14, 1978).   The Assembly
decided "to consider at a later stage the feasibility
of observing an international year of the elderly."
(Res. 33/52, para. 2).   In 1980, the General Assembly changed the name to the World Assembly on Aging
"in view of the interrelatedness of the aging of
individuals and the aging of populations..." (Res.
35/129, adopted December 11, 1980).   The World Assembly was later scheduled for July 26 to August 6,
1982 in Vienna. (See General Assembly Res. 36/30,
adopted November 13, 1981.)

In a preview of the 1982 World Assembly on Aging,
Margaret Kelly, a United Nations Secretariat official,
asserted that "full participation and full integration

of older adults into society would most likely be a
major theme." She pointed out that those over 60
years of age are the fastest growing segment of
society. "In 1971, there were 291 million people
in the world over age 60 and this figure will increase by 100 percent by the year 2000 to 582 million
older. The increase will be most pronounced in the
developing world," she asserted. (Preview of the
World Assembly on the Elderly, Office of Public
Information, Nongovernmental Organizations Section,
United Nations, DPI/NGO/SB/79/35, May 1, 1979).

As plans developed for the World Assembly on
Aging (originally titled World Assembly on the
Elderly), nongovernmental organization committees
were formed at New York City and Vienna. The
Committees were accorded official status with relation to the Conference of NGO's (CONGO) in consulta-
tive status with the United Nations Economic and
Social Council (ECOSOC). They have helped to shape
the deliberations leading up to the World Assembly
and of declarations likely to be adopted at the
Assembly. Committee members were active in a Forum
of nongovernmental organizations for the World Assembly on Aging in Vienna held in that city March 29
to April 2, 1982. The Forum was sponsored by the
International Centre on Social Gerontology, Paris.
Mr. L. Brisson of the Centre served as Executive
Secretary of the Forum and Mr. J. Flesch, also of
the Centre, as Chairman of the Forum Organizing
Committee as well as of the Forum itself. Officers
of the New York based NGO Committee on Aging are:
Lt. Col. Mary E. Verner, Salvation Army, Chairper-
son; Margaret Berdard, International Catholic Child
Guidance Bureau, Vice-chairperson; Lorraine Jablon-
ski, United Neighborhood Houses, Secretary; Sylvia
Kleinman, Gray Panthers, Treasurer. Ms. Kleinman,
who furnished the foregoing information on the New
York committee, can be reached at 188 Fifth Avenue,
Norwood, New Jersey, 07648, or at telephone (201)
767-3125. The Vienna-based committee is chaired by
Monica Tupay, International Federation for Home Eco-
nomics, Bundesseminar fur das Lanwirtschaftliche
Bildungswesen Angermayergasse 1 1130 Vienna.

United Nations Secretariat activities with respect to aging are coordinated from the Centre for
Social Development and Humanitarian Affairs, Vienna
International Centre, P.O. Box 500, A-1400, Vienna,
Austria. The Centre, while located in Vienna, is
a unit of the Department of International Economic
and Social Affairs, itself based at New York City,
at United Nations headquarters.

An important document pertaining to the World
Assembly on Aging was issued in late June of 1982
under the title Report of the Advisory Committee on
the World Assembly on the Aging in its Third Session,
Vienna, 3-7 May 1982 (United Nations document A/Conf
113/24, June 25, 1982). See also report to the Secretary General of the United Nations on the Nongovernmental Organization Forum for the World Assembly on
the Aging, Vienna, March 29-April 2, 1982. This
report, prepared by Mr. J. Flesch, Forum Chairperson,
can be obtained from the International Centre on
Social Gerontology, 91 Rue Jouffrey, 75017, Paris,
France.

174